Nell Brooker Mayhew

Paintings on Paper

Published in the United States of America 2005

Editing: Jesse Brink
Design: Distinc Design
Print Production: Navigator Cross-media

For information address
Balcony Press
512 E. Wilson Suite 213
Glendale, California 91206

Library of Congress Catalog Card Number: 2002103808
ISBN 1-890449-16-4
Printed in Korea

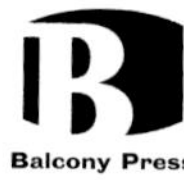

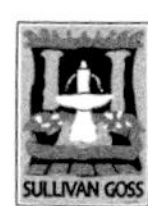

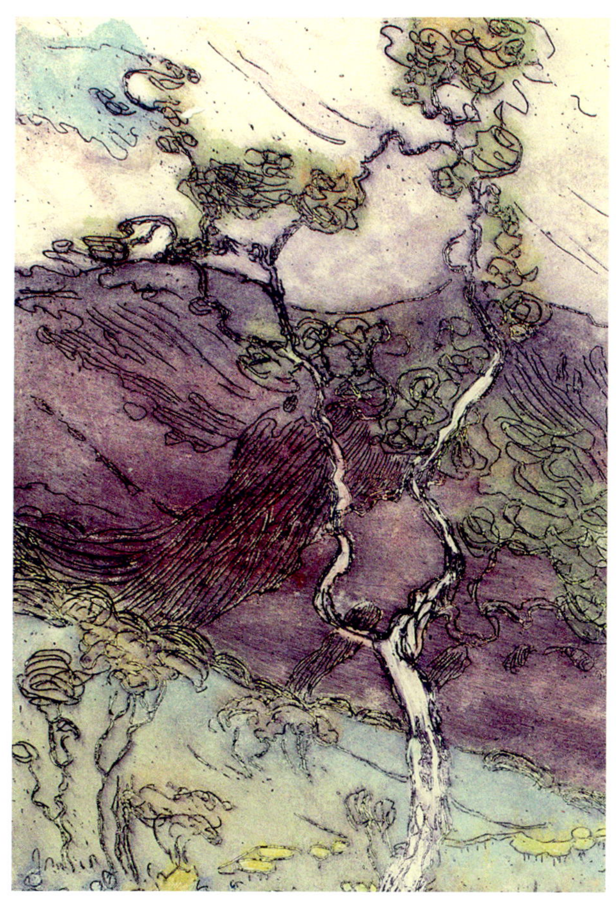

Nell Brooker Mayhew

Paintings on Paper

by Alissa J. Anderson | Research by Gloria Rexford Martin

Balcony Press, Los Angeles | Sullivan Goss, Santa Barbara

"Color etching is this generation's contribution to art . . .
it has always meant to me an opportunity to express the
glowing atmospheric color of American landscape in a
medium exquisite and aristocratic, but yet a print—and
because it is a print—a democratic thing—belonging to all."

— Nell Brooker Mayhew

Introduction

Nell Brooker Mayhew, an American artist trained in the Midwest, brought a bold and bright new spirit to the Southern California art scene. With color and energy as her tools, Mayhew quickly established herself as a noteworthy artist, speaker and teacher among a freethinking Los Angeles art crowd. When she arrived, at the turn of the nineteenth century, the Arts and Crafts movement was in its prime and Nell Brooker Mayhew placed herself at the center of activity. During her l ifetime, she exhibited in California, New York and Chicago. Mayhew was a respected California artist, and yet her acclaim would not endure.

Ambitious and energetic, Mayhew was well established in both the art and academic worlds. She had received her training from the Art Institute of Chicago and became a faculty member of the College of Fine Arts at the University of Southern California Garvanza campus. She lived in the Arroyo Seco section of Pasadena, which was a sanctuary for Plein Air artists such as Hanson Puthuff, Jean Mannheim and Elmer Wachtel. Mayhew was a staple in this artists' colony, working and exhibiting with major Southern California artists, including Edgar Payne, William Judson and the Gearhart sisters. Her oil paintings and color etchings were often displayed in local, national and international exhibitions, and discussed in prominent art magazines.

Although best known for her boldly colored, expressive oil paintings, Mayhew's color etchings are perhaps her most entrancing works. Pioneering her own process of printmaking, she took etching beyond the black and white model made famous by German printmaker Albrecht Dürer. Her colored prints borrowed concepts from age-old etching techniques, but also incorporated color into the traditional monotype process. Mayhew stood at the forefront of artistic innovation with a collection that she called, "paintings on paper." These works were distinct from the artistic practices of her day. Inspired by nature, they incorporated stylistic elements drawn from Japanese prints, Arts and Crafts handiwork and French Symbolist paintings.

Mayhew's wide-ranging exposure dwindled rapidly after her death in 1940. Unlike many of her contemporaries, she has received little recent recognition beyond mentions in reference books. Without a dealer or celebrated collector to promote her work, no one cultivated her contribution to American art. The heirs to Mayhew's estate, treasuring her work, have kept their pieces out of public circulation, increasing her obscurity. The public and critics have not had the opportunity to see her paintings or etchings for decades. This slim volume endeavors to lessen her obscurity and return the artist and her works to the level of renown and respect that they once enjoyed.

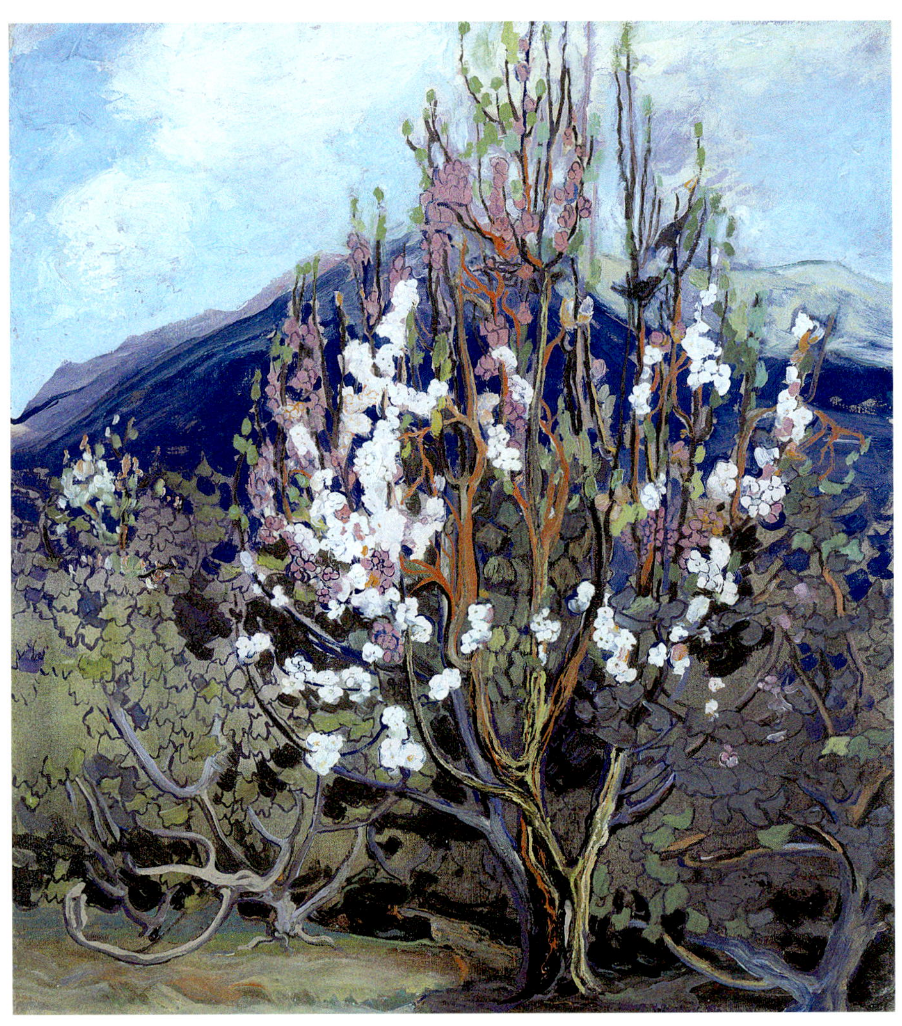

Tree in Bloom
n.d., Oil on canvas, 32" x 28"
Collection of Frank and Patricia Goss

Biography

Nell Brooker Mayhew was born in Astoria, Illinois, in 1875. Given the name Nell Cole Danely at birth, she was the first of five children born to Reverend Alfred Danely and his wife, Ella. As a Methodist minister, Alfred was summoned to change congregations every six years. Thus the family moved frequently, finally settling in Urbana, Illinois. Nellie, as she was known as a child, otherwise lived a typical Midwestern childhood. Starting at an early age, she began drawing and painting.[1] By 1892, at the age of sixteen, she had exhibited her first watercolor, "Yacht," at the Art Institute of Chicago's Annual Exhibition of Watercolors by American Artists.[2] This was a notable achievement for someone of her age and gender.

With the support of her parents, she decided to attend Northwestern University. Taking only three years to graduate, she received a Bachelor of Science, in 1897. Because Northwestern did not offer an art program, she began her post-graduate work at Chicago University, now known as University of Chicago.[3] From 1901-1906 Mayhew did further post-graduate work at the University of Illinois, Champaign Urbana. There she studied with Newton A. Wells, who was a painter, sculptor and architect trained in Paris.[4] It is likely that Wells brought knowledge of Degas' innovative black-and-white monotypes back to the school, and shared it with his students. Degas was strongly influenced by the Japonisme movement and eventually became recognized as the primary innovator of black-and-white monotypes. His experimentation with monotypes from 1875-1885 sparked an entire movement among turn-of-the-century artists.[5] It was as Wells' pupil that Mayhew began pioneering the color etching process that would become her trademark.[6]

While studying at the University of Illinois, Mayhew met Sidney Brooker, editor of the Quincy, Illinois, newspaper. The young couple was married in 1902, in a double wedding with Mayhew's sister Adelaide. Their father conducted the ceremony. Tragically, heart failure unexpectedly struck the young man six months after their wedding. Mayhew was forever saddened by the loss of her first husband and greatest love. After his passing, Mayhew continued to incorporate the name 'Brooker' into her signature in tribute to him.

Despite her sadness, Mayhew continued her pursuit of an art career. In 1905, two years after Sidney's death, she enrolled at the Art Institute of Chicago. While attending the Art Institute, Mayhew studied under Danish painter John Johansen. Known for his impressionist and tonalist paintings, Johansen had studied at the Academie Julian, in Paris, and at James Whistler's Academie Carmen.[7] Johansen was deeply interested in the atmospheric effects of light in his scene painting. He often painted landscapes and interior scenes demonstrating tonalist influences. For instance, during his tour of Europe, Johansen's cityscapes of Venice are painted in such a manner that the buildings appear to merge into sky — a result of his monochromatic use of a yellow and orange tonalist palette. Mayhew's style would eventually stray from Johansen's traditional technique, but her work would

[1] Steve Turner and Victoria Dailey, *Nell Brooker Mayhew: Color Etchings and Paintings* (Los Angeles: Turner Dailey Gallery, 1989), 3-5. /[2] Peter Hastings Falk, ed., *Annual Exhibition Record of the Art Institute of Chicago 1888-1950* (Madison, CT: Sound View Press, 1990). /[3] Tyler Sullivan Goss, *Nell Brooker Mayhew: Master of the Color Etching and California Painter* (Santa Barbara, CA: Sullivan Goss, Ltd., circa 2002). /[4] Glenn Opitz, ed., *Mantle Fielding's Dictionary of American Painters,* 2nd ed. (Poughkeepsie, NY: Apollo, 1986), 1010. /[5] The Metropolitan Museum of Art, *The Painterly Print* (New York: The Metropolitan Museum of Art, 1981), 30. /[6] Northwestern University Archives, "Northwestern University Record of Alumni Accomplishments," 1-5. /[7] "John Johanson biography," *AskArt.com* (AskArt.com, n.d.), www.askart.com/biography.asp.

forever reference his landscape-based scenes and impressionist influence.

For a short time, Mayhew studied under muralist and painter John Vanderpoel, also an instructor at the Art Institute. Vanderpoel, who was also Georgia O'Keeffe's mentor, was a painter, born in the Netherlands, who eventually settled in Chicago. He authored the book, *The Human Figure*, which served as an important text for the teaching of figurative painting.[8] While Mayhew's work from this early period is largely missing, she learned classical figurative draftsmanship while studying under Vanderpoel. From him, Mayhew also learned the technique of mural painting.[9] Vanderpoel helped Mayhew lay the groundwork of tradition from which she would eventually develop her own style.

Trained by Vanderpoel, Johansen and Wells, Mayhew was earning the credentials she needed to become a successful artist. But, rather than adopting the traditional and conventional techniques of her instructors, she began implementing her own bold and loose painting style. Mayhew's strong character was forming, as was her technique. Mayhew's eldest daughter, Mary Jane Barton once said: "She was her own artist. She wasn't influenced by anyone. She was very much an individual."[10] Simply pursuing a career in art was itself a progressive act. Typically, only those women who were financially privileged and extraordinarily talented could apply to the major art schools. Even then, many were turned down, but Mayhew was persistent.

After completing her studies at the Art Institute of Chicago, in 1908, Mayhew moved to Los Angeles. The artist headed west in hopes of beginning a new life untainted by the tragedy of her husband's death. Although Los Angeles was not yet the center for entertainment it would become, the coastal milieu had spurred a growing artist colony. Art schools were burgeoning in the largely rural Los Angeles landscape, and a community of progressive artists was crafting the first examples of California Impressionism. Mayhew found inspiration in the West Coast environs. Her father accompanied her to California, helping her settle in the Arroyo Seco area now known as Highland Park where she built a house and studio. She had her heavy etching press shipped by boat around Cape Horn, at the tip of South America.[11] Once the press arrived, she began her new life as a California artist in earnest.

Mayhew had her first Los Angeles solo exhibition, mere months after her arrival, at the Blanchard Gallery in November 1908. The exhibit received a particularly harsh review from a critic with *The Graphic,* a weekly Los Angeles newspaper. He commends her technique but characterizes Mayhew's work thusly: "Mrs. Nell Danely Brooker's [work] betrays a great insincerity of purpose. If [her pieces] had gained any point for the furtherance of an expression of art in any form it would be excusable, but they have gained nothing."[12] The abrasive review did not hinder Mayhew. She continued to establish herself in the Los Angeles art scene, winning a bronze medal for her color etching "Sand Dunes," at the Alaska-Yukon Exposition, less than a year later.[13]

[8] "John Vanderpoel biography," *AskArt.com* (AskArt.com, n.d.), www.askart.com/biography.asp. /[9] Years later, in 1937, she completed a mural for the Ashton Public Library, in Illinois. Northwestern University Archives, "Northwestern University Record of Alumni Accomplishments," 1-5. /[10] Mary Jane Barton and Nell Kemble, interviewed by Alissa Anderson, Santa Barbara, CA, April/May 2003. /[11] Steve Turner and Victoria Dailey, *Nell Brooker Mayhew: Color Etchings and Paintings* (Los Angeles: Turner Dailey Gallery, 1989), 1-3. /[12] Rene T. De Quelin, "Art and Artists," *(Los Angeles) Graphic,* 7 Nov 1908. /[13] Alaska Yukon-Pacific Exhibition, *Fine Arts Gallery and Exhibit of Arts and Crafts* (Seattle: n.p., 1909).

In 1910, Mayhew became a faculty member at the College of Fine Arts at the Garvanza campus of the University of Southern California in Pasadena. There she taught a class on "outdoor sketching". The dean of the school was William Lees Judson, a prominent artist in the area. Judson and Mayhew were often mentioned in joint exhibitions in the *Los Angeles Times* "Art and Artists" column. In one article, the critic first discusses Judson's atmospheric seascapes after which he analyzes Mayhew's work. Calling her technique "bright, brave, happy," he commends Mayhew for her unrefined, innovative style. Her distinctive brushstrokes are loose and gestural. The *Los Angeles Times'* primary art critic, Arthur Anderson, described Mayhew's irreverant nature: "The painter has left her canvas bare in spots and very successfully, utterly unmindful (as she would temperamentally and consistently be) of the old, time-honored, art school mandate: Cover the canvas!"[14]

To have appeared in a joint exhibition with the famous Judson was quite an achievement, but Mayhew soon outshone Judson. In *The Graphic's* 1910 review of the USC College of Fine Art opening, critic Everett C. Maxwell only briefly mentions Judson's work before focusing his attention on Mayhew. He notes that Judson's works are "several of his best efforts." But of Mayhew, he writes: "Of great interest are the examples of impressionist art shown by Nell Danely Brooker, whose work in oils is rapidly winning favor for this talented young woman, not only locally but in the East as well."[15] In the following week's review of the show, Maxwell devotes an entire full-page review to Mayhew alone.

Mayhew began to exhibit regularly. The coming years would be her most productive. She participated in exhibitions on a yearly basis over the next two decades. Her solo shows received wide attention from the local art critics, such as Anthony Anderson, of the *Times*. He commended Mayhew's color etchings for their likeness to oil paintings. His support helped legitimize Mayhew's progressive works: "Endowed with a fine sense for decorative values in line, mass, and color, she brings the same art intelligence to her work . . . Now and again you are perplexed to know whether you are looking at a painting or a print."[16]

Mayhew was also celebrated for her handling of color and light. In a 1910 article, in *The Graphic*, critic Maxwell writes: "The relation of objects is wonderfully felt, and the value and harmony of color is unerring in quality. A panel of eucalyptus is a revelation in the handling of sunlight and shadow and possesses much real truth."[17] One year later, Maxwell once again commends the artist, calling her work "daring almost to a danger point." He continues, "She is first and foremost a decorator of rare attainment and after that a colorist and a designer of ability . . . The composition is superbly decorative and the color is lovely."[18]

Meanwhile, although the artist was busy developing her career, she also began a new family, marrying attorney-by-trade, poet-by-passion, Leonard Mayhew in 1911. She also gave birth to daughter Mary Jane that year. Nell followed, in 1914. Being a mother did not stifle her ambitions or lessen her productive energies. She was rapidly

[14] Arthur Anderson, "Art and Artists," *Los Angeles Times*, 21 May 1911, 20. /[15] Everett C. Maxwell, "Art," *(Los Angeles) Graphic*, 8 Oct 1910, 9. /[16] Arthur Anderson, "Art and Artists," *Los Angeles Times*, 20 Oct 1912, 19. /[17] Everett C. Maxwell, "Art," *(Los Angeles) Graphic*, 22 Oct 1910, 9. /[18] Everett C. Maxwell, "Art," *(Los Angeles) Graphic*, 27 May 1911, 9.

gaining national recognition. Harriet Monroe of the *Chicago Tribune* called Mayhew's work an imaginative interpretation of the color-etching medium. The critic goes on to write, "Always her touch is light and sure; she expresses her theme with grace and a certain eloquence."[19]

Mayhew continued to develop her technique and achieve acclaim throughout the teens. "April Morn" and "Sand Dunes," in 1917, and "Blue and Gold" and "Happy Valley," in 1919, became exemplary models of her technique.[20] In the latter part of the decade, the artist began her studies for the California Mission color etchings. This series is perhaps Mayhew's most highly regarded group of pieces. To create the works, she and her daughters drove almost the entire length of California so she could make sketches of all twenty-one of the remaining Spanish missions. Mayhew described her trip: "It is a thrilling experience to follow along the old trail on which stood the old Missions of California — the first highway on the Pacific Coast — a trail thru the wildflowers and luxuriant growth — following the ocean from the south to the north of California."[21]

She reminisced: "When first I was intrigued into making a tour of the missions, I thought it might become a bit tiresome for I expected to find the same architectural plan executed for each mission. Imagine my delight at being entirely mistaken. No two missions are alike; each one was built by the plan needed for the particular location. It seems as if there had been the artist's joy in creating each design a new idea . . ."[22] Returning home with the sketches, Mayhew would finish the drawings in the studio. She would spend countless hours etching the drawings, and then printing them on the handmade papers sent to her by a cousin in Wisconsin. She often experimented with printing the designs in a wide variety of color themes.

In tandem with her active exhibition schedule, Mayhew also accepted commissions. One of her most important came in 1921, when she was asked to provide the newly built Ambassador Hotel in Los Angeles with 108 of her color etchings. In a review by the *Los Angeles Times*, much of the charm of the hotel is attributed to her artwork. In the same year, ninety-four of Mayhew's pieces were sent to New York's Ambassador Hotel.

She also found time for journalism, writing an article for the February 1925 issue of *California Southland*. In the piece, entitled "Prints for the Small House," she argues for the importance of art in the home. The artist challenged the common belief that art was too expensive for the average household: "Well, perhaps one should not care if [artwork is expensive], since also a radio, a piano, an automobile, are expensive, and yet they are likely to appear in a small house . . . One buys what one really wants. It is really wanting it that counts."[23] Mayhew goes on to make the remarkable claim that color etchings are of greater value than traditional oil paintings: "In the first place no oil painting can be more exquisite than a beautiful etching or block-print. Anyone who has informed himself at all about pictures, loves an etching, the aristocrat among pictures."[24]

Her energy and business sense were tested by the dissolution of her marriage in the 1920s. Although Mayhew had built her career as an independent woman,

[19] Arthur Anderson, "Poetic Interpretations," *Los Angeles Times,* 7 Dec 1913, 7. /[20] Raymond L. Wilson, *Index of American Print Exhibitions, 1882-1940* (Metuchen, NJ and London: The Scarecrow Press, Inc., 1988), 61, 81, 197, 200, 216, 755.
/[21] Steve Turner and Victoria Dailey, *Nell Brooker Mayhew: Color Etchings and Paintings* (Los Angeles: Turner Dailey Gallery, 1989), 4.
/[22] *Ibid.* /[23] Nell Brooker Mayhew, "Prints for the Small House," *California Southland,* February 1925, 22. /[24] *Ibid.*

it was difficult to be a single mother in the years of the Depression. She augmented her income in a variety of ways. "She had to," said daughter Mary Jane Barton. "She had no choice, she had the two of us to feed. I remember one week we only had soup to eat."[25] Trading her works for services like dentistry and doctor's appointments, the artist found innovative ways of supporting her children. She often gave painting lessons to private students in her home. She also opened her own gallery in West Hollywood where she exhibited her work along with other artists and craftsmen of the area. In 1930, Mayhew participated in Purchase Prize Exhibit, in Gardena, California, alongside Hanson Puthuff and Edgar Payne.

Going still further, Mayhew began an art rental business where one could rent fine art. During the Depression this allowed for a temporary, cheaper alternative for patrons to support their favorite artists. Mayhew's art business was innovative enough to end up on the front-page of the *Los Angeles Examiner*: "The picture renting plan allows the Los Angeles art lover to have a much wider selection of paintings in his home than if he had to buy them, and if he tires of one picture, after living with it for a while, he may return it and take another, perhaps better suited to his mood."[26]

In the midst of all this work, Mayhew injured her leg, leading to the onset of phlebitis, a painful circulatory problem in the limbs. She was also diagnosed with anemia, an ailment causing her extreme fatigue. Mayhew's active lifestyle became immediately threatened. Although art and gardening were her greatest passions, they became more and more difficult for her to pursue. The artist continued working in her studio and garden, but for much shorter periods of time. Nell Brooker Mayhew remained active until her death, at age 65, on September 24, 1940.[27]

[25] Mary Jane Barton and Nell Kemble, interviewed by Alissa Anderson, Santa Barbara, CA, April/May 2003. /[26] "Art Renting Plan Approved," *Los Angeles Examiner*, 18 Jan 1931, 1. /[27] Edan Milton Hughes, *Artists in California: 1786 – 1940*, vol. 2 (San Francisco: Hughes Publishing Company, 1989), 363.

Influences

The Arts and Crafts movement, a late nineteenth century artistic philosophy focused on the importance of nature, quality craftsmanship and artistic involvement, heavily influenced Mayhew. Sparked by the rapid onset of the machine age, and given voice by the writings of John Ruskin and William Morris, the Arts and Crafts movement emphasized the importance of hand-made objects. Art scholar Wendy Kaplan describes the movement: "The integration of physical and mental labor and the recognition that art is a source for regeneration available to all was the basic ideology of turn-of-the-century reformers."[28] Art for everyday life, decoration, high quality materials and personal creation were the objectives of the Arts and Crafts artists. Ultimately, those who defined themselves as Arts and Crafts artists felt there had to be a unity between art and production—not a division between the two.

The contemporaneous Aesthetic movement, with its philosophy of "art for art's sake," also influenced Mayhew. The Aesthetic movement declared a correlation between beautiful, hand-made surroundings and the quality of life, rejecting the reductive effects of industrialization. Its practitioners believed that beautiful objects could bring inspiration to everyone, not just the privileged.[29] Many people were receptive to this idea and were interested in information on how to decorate the home. Mayhew herself was often asked to give lectures, discussing topics on the importance of art in the home and how to place art in museums. Mary Jane Barton, Mayhew's eldest daughter, said of her mother: "She believed in beauty, period."[30]

Mayhew's color etchings are also highly reminiscent of the Japonisme style — a term conceived in France, in 1872, to define a taste for Japanese culture. With the opening of Japan, in the 1850s, the Western world became intrigued by the mystique of the ancient Orient.[31] Japanese printmaking came to embody the Arts and Craft model: ideals focused on nature, simplicity and spirituality. Japanese printmakers were regarded for "their refinement, their brilliant and powerful execution, and subtle compositions."[32] Many of Mayhew's scenes are reminiscent of Japanese motifs. Her use of high horizon lines, simple scenes of nature and a vertical, columnar style are typical of Japanese pillar prints.

Mayhew's experimentation led her to investigate other styles as well. She embraced color variations and borrowed themes from a variety of artistic movements. Her piece "California Poppies," for example, shows a rare Symbolist ethic. In this instance, Mayhew's palette shifts to a more muted, tonalist approach used by principal Symbolists like Odilon Redon. The objects in "California Poppies" have a subtle atmospheric effect captured in a whimsical, almost lyrical manner. "The style was refined, elegant, subtle, intellectual . . . Symbolists found the creation of a mood to be as important as the transmission of information, and sought to engage the entire mind and personality of the viewer by appealing to the viewer's emotions and unconscious mind as well as intellect."[33]

Mayhew's work also, at times, reflected the Impressionist movement developing in California. *The Graphic's* Everett C. Maxwell writes, in 1910: "There has

[28] Wendy Kaplan, *The Art That is Life* (Boston: Museum of Fine Arts, 1987), 52. / [29] "The Aesthetic Movement" (n.p., 29 June 2003), www.webdesk.com/quotations/aes.html. / [30] Mary Jane Barton and Nell Kemble, interviewed by Alissa Anderson, Santa Barbara, CA, April/May 2003. / [31] Julia Meech and Gabriel P. Wisberg, *Japonisme Comes to America: The Japanese Impact on Graphic Arts 1876–1925* (New York: Harry N. Abrams, Inc. 1990), 7. / [32] Nancy E Green, "Arthur Wesley Dow: American Arts and Crafts," *American Art Review*, Nov/Dec 1999, 220. / [33] "The Symbolist Movement – An Introduction" (Boston: Boston College, n.d.), www.bc.edu/bc_org/avp/cas/fnart/symbolist/symbolist_intro.html. In a sense Paul Gauguin's relief carving Soyez Mysterieuses (1890) sums up this goal of the Symbolist movement. See H.R. Rookmaaker, *Gauguin and 19th Century Art Theory* (Amsterdam: n.p., 1972), 220-224 and Vojtech Jirat-Wasiutynski, Gauguin in the Context of Symbolism (New York: n.p., 1976).

not been very much good impressionistic work accomplished. It is as yet an undeveloped field, but its followers are serious-minded people, seekers after broader truths . . . Of our several local art workers . . . who have the courage of their convictions, there is no one more enthusiastic, or more worthy of serious consideration, than Nell Danely Brooker."[34] Nevertheless Mayhew never fully embraced Impressionism. Like the Impressionist artists, her images of nature attempted to capture the essence of sensation — not traditional realism. But art, for Mayhew, went beyond appearance to explore expression, reflection and interpretation.

The spontaneity with which she painted was central to understanding her distinct approach to art. In both her oil paintings, as well as her color etchings, Mayhew was disinterested in precision of line. The artist painted a number of oil paintings reflecting an Expressionist ethic. Mayhew was concerned with concepts of movement and painterly expression as means to poetic interpretation. As she said herself: "The grandeur of the West cannot be painted in detail and the chief aim of art is decoration, hence my canvases will be mere notes of form and color, yet they must sing with light and air."[35] Her oil paintings aim to evoke spirit and emotion — resisting accuracy and aesthetic precision.

Independent of style, nature was deeply embedded in Mayhew's concept of art, as well as life. It stood continually as her strongest inspiration, and ultimately her greatest influence. Capturing "the grandeur of the West" was the sole intent of her art. She savored all elements of nature, capturing each detail in her oil paintings. She attempted to depict even the most subtle elements in each landscape including dead weeds and lifeless trees. In a 1911 review by *The Graphic,* Mayhew is commended for her attention to nature: "Nature is to her eye a pattern of lines and a mosaic of glorious color. She paints the sensations of nature without becoming sensational in her art."[36]

Mayhew knew precisely how to extract from nature its purest attributes. Glowing with color and movement, her art captures the swirling energy of life. "One can feel the same decorative rhythm of cloud and tree and mountain — for so it is that every artist interprets Nature each in his own way. A picture is a message from one soul to another."[37] An avid gardener throughout her life, she was also one of California's early conservationists. She expressed her environmental stance directly and succinctly: "We need beauty to influence our mental and moral existence just as much as we require bread and butter for a physical development."[38]

34 Everett C. Maxwell, "Art," *(Los Angeles) Graphic,* 22 Oct 1910, 9. /35 *Ibid.* /36 Everett C. Maxwell, "Art," *(Los Angeles) Graphic,* 27 May 1911, 9. /37 Nell Brooker Mayhew, *Nell Brooker Mayhew; Painter, Etcher* (n.p., n.d.). /38 Nell Brooker Mayhew, "Letters to the Editor," *Los Angeles Times,* 14 Apr 1916, 5.

Technique

Mayhew chose to unite organic themes of nature with a new process of handmade etching. Here she could incorporate high-quality materials, personal craftsmanship and simple decoration to create unique pieces of art from a repetitive process of reproduction. For Mayhew, fine art was not contradictory to craft. Instead, the two became synonymous. Nature, as expressed in the delicate craft of printmaking, was the essence of her work.

Printmaking, as practiced by members of the Arts and Crafts movement, was immediately derived from Japanese Ukiyo-e prints. In these traditional Japanese woodblock prints, an artist would design the picture, a craftsman would create the carving and the publisher would create the final print. Arts and Crafts innovators removed the division of labor in the Japanese process. Printmaker Roi Partridge described the new approach: "Etchings are made in curious and interesting ways, in which the virtues of the craftsman are mingled with the intuition and sensitivity of the artist.[39]

Mayhew's process of printmaking came to embody a signature style all her own, merging the traditional black-and-white etching technique with the monotype process of the 19th century. Mayhew drew from these previous models, yet innovated a new type of color-etching process, employing a two-step method. First, she etched her design into a waxed copper plate. She then printed the waxed plate in black, dark blue, or brown ink, and allowed the initial print to set overnight.[40] Once the ink had set, she applied her colorful oils to the original copper plate and re-printed over the previous impressions.

Mayhew would make multiple colored prints with the same plate, using varied levels of saturation. Often, she would wipe the plate clean and re-ink in a different color theme. Although each print was derived from the same outline, variations created unique and distinctive motifs. They typically share a distinct luminosity that was a direct result of her technique: "Transfer of the oil onto the paper in a very thin layer imparts two other traits to the medium: those are a flatness of surface and a pervasive luminosity, the latter [is] a result of the visibility of the underlying paper, which casts light through the pigment."[41]

Understanding Mayhew's unique color etching style is necessary to understanding her work. She combines the painterly essence of monotypes with the craft-based etching process. The prints become individual "paintings on paper" instead of multiple, uniform copies. The same plate was often inked to create the impression of a spring morning and then re-inked to look like a fall evening. Each piece becomes a unique, modified representation of the same scene. Mayhew had no interest in regulated, homogenized reproductions.

Mayhew's prints challenged the norms of color etching, creating artwork more like paintings than typical prints. "In color etchings she stands pre-eminent. The beauty of her paintings is more than merely decorative. It has singing poetic suggestion."[42]

[39] Roi Partridge, "The Art and Craft of Etching," *The Argus: A Journal of Art*, July/August 1928, 4-5. /[40] Steve Turner and Victoria Dailey, *Nell Brooker Mayhew: Color Etchings and Paintings* (Los Angeles: Turner Dailey Gallery, 1989), 4. /[41] Cecily Langdale, *Monotypes by Maurice Prendergast in the Terra Museum of American Art* (Chicago: The Terra Museum of American Art, 1984), 21. /[42] "Nell Brooker Mayhew." *The Western Woman*, March 1939, 58.

Conclusion

Nell Brooker Mayhew was a progressive woman and a progressive artist. She defied the artistic traditions around her, advocating a new process of printmaking and a new style of painting embracing color, freedom of brushstroke and, above all — Nature. The result of her efforts was a substantial body of work steeped in innovation, aesthetic precision and creative insight.

But, after her death, Mayhew's work was rarely exhibited. During the 1940s and 1950s the Arts and Crafts movement fell out of favor. Modernists disparaged the work of artists like Mayhew as too literal, sentimental and representational. It is not until the last decade that her work has been rediscovered. Over three hundred original works exist as reflections of Mayhew's significant body of work and artistic accomplishment.

"She thought there should be no limit to art, to what was beautiful."[43]

[43] Mary Jane Barton and Nell Kemble, interviewed by Alissa Anderson, Santa Barbara, CA, April/May 2003. As stated by Mary Jane Barton.

Unless otherwise noted, all artwork part of the collection of Sullivan Goss — An American Gallery

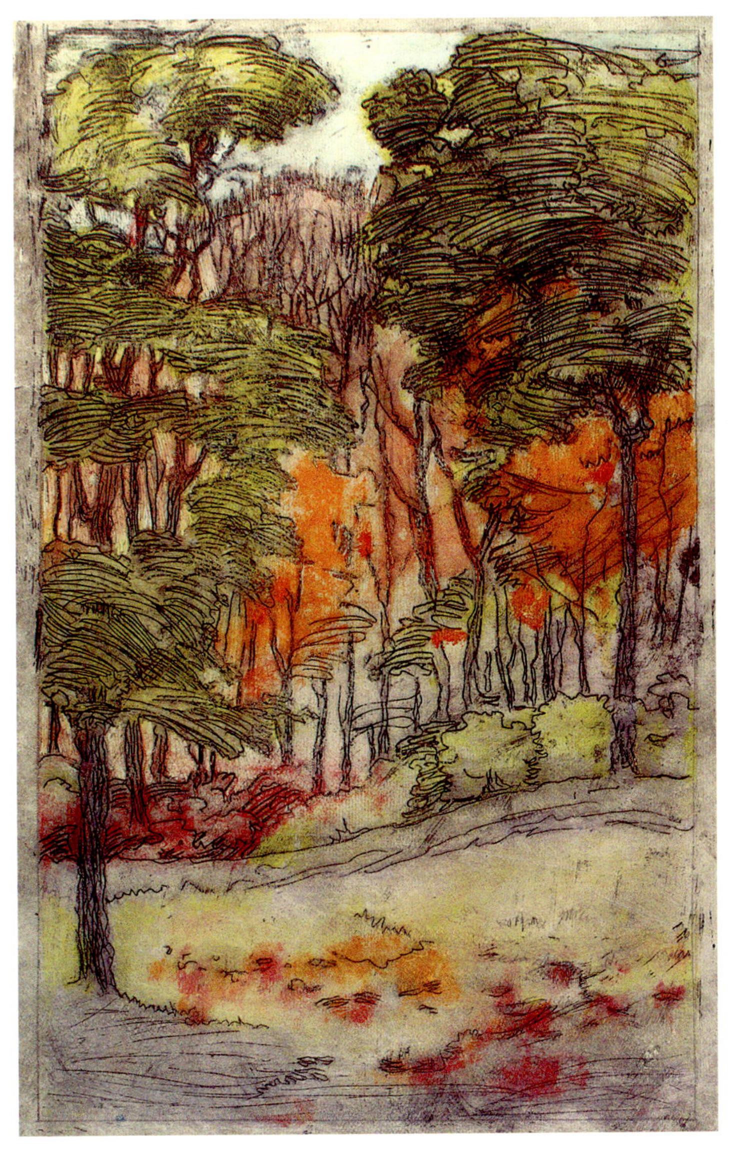

Eucalyptus Grove
n.d., Color etching, 21.5" x 13"

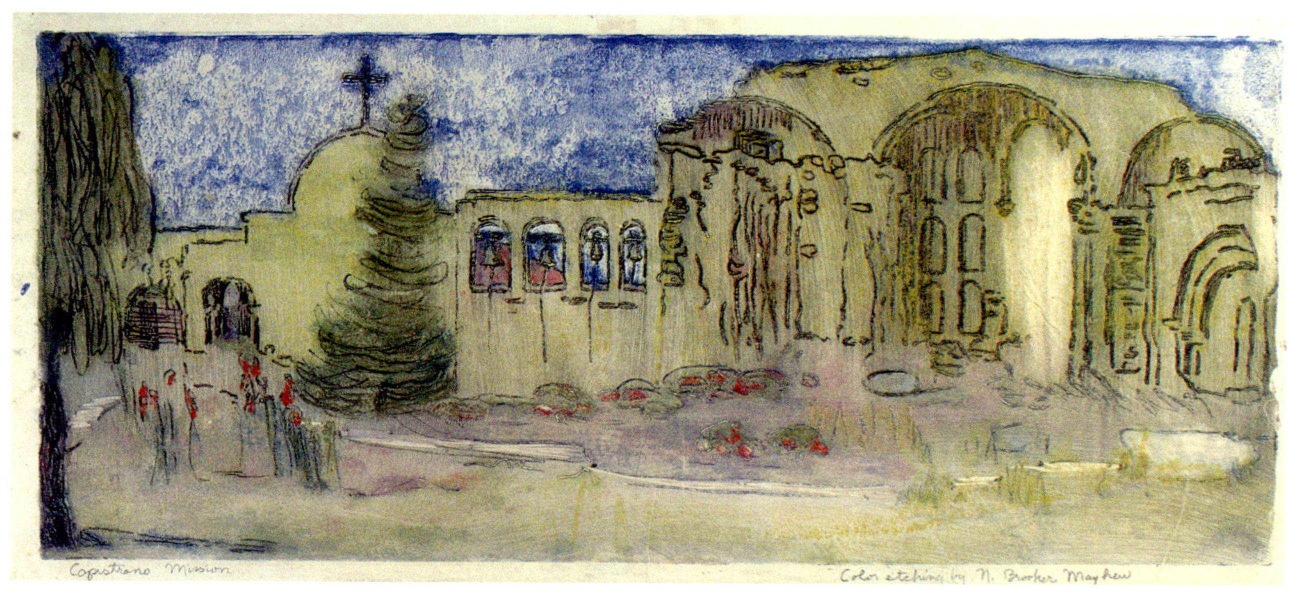

Capistrano Mission
c. 1920s, Color etching, 9" x 20.5"

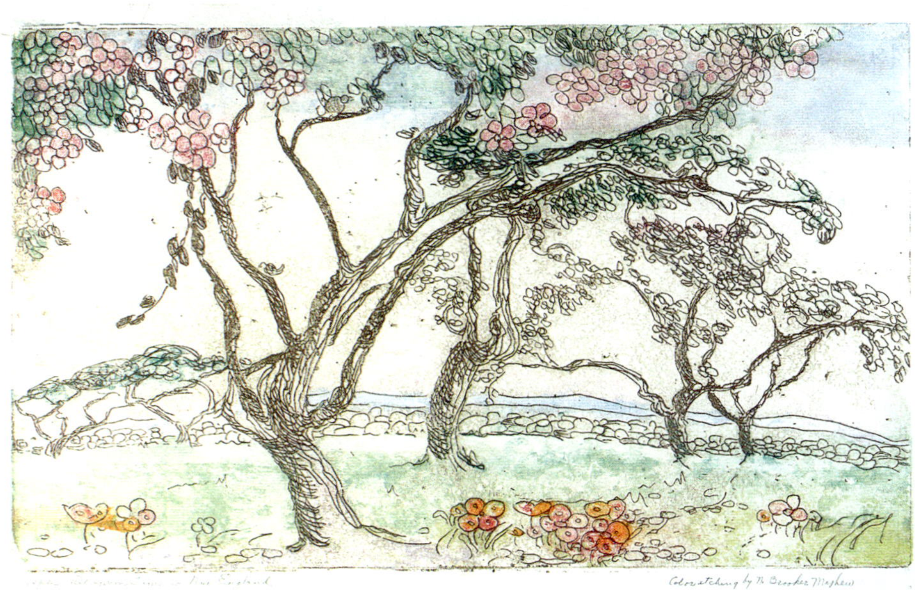

Apple Blossom Time in New England
c. 1920s, Color etching, 11" x 18"

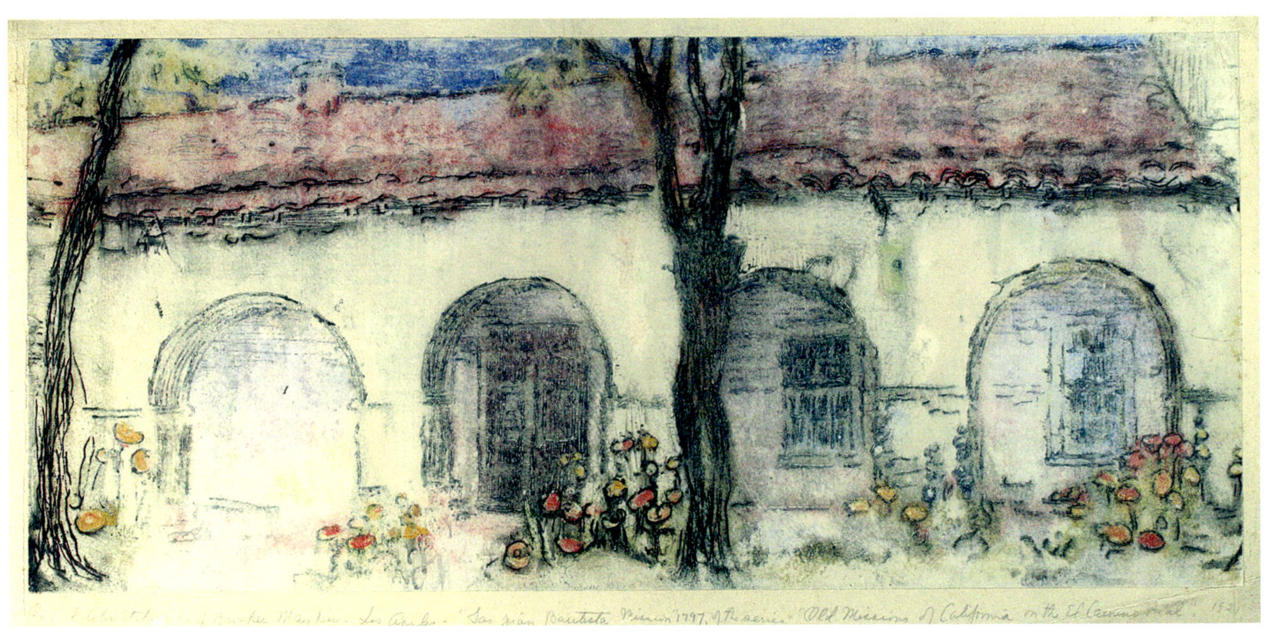

San Juan Bautista Mission
1921, Color etching, 10.75" x 23.25"

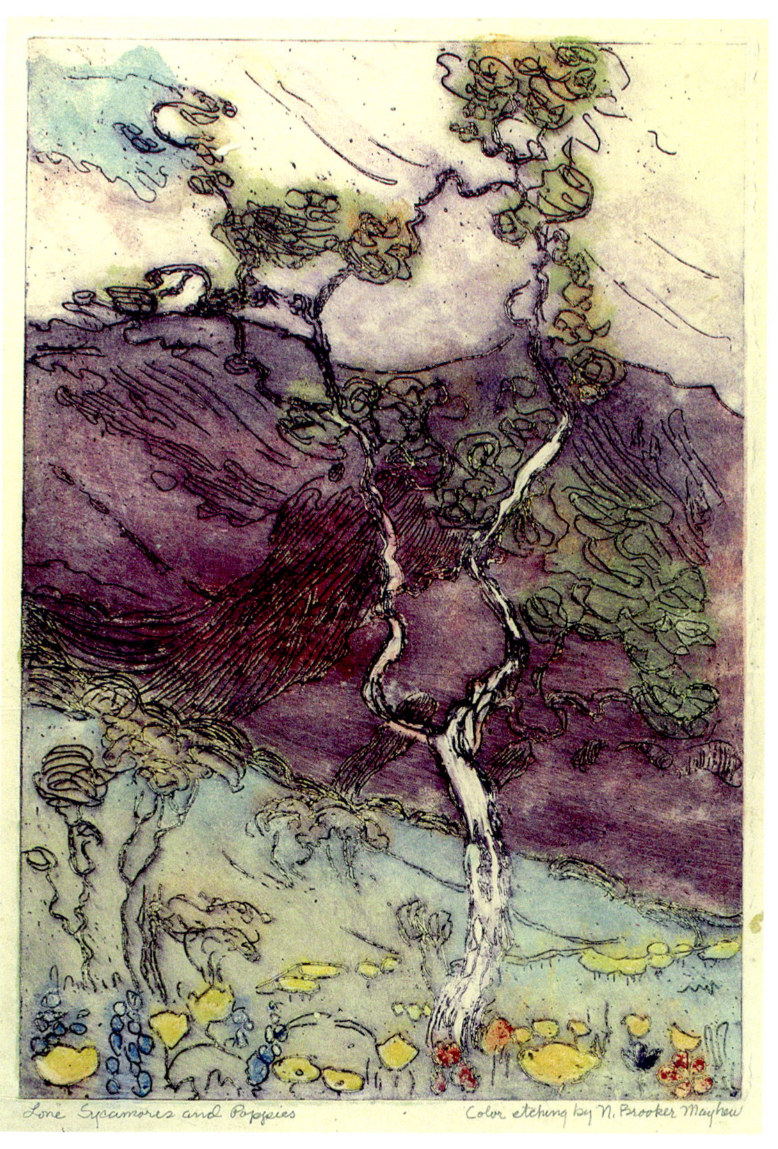

Lone Sycamores and Poppies
n.d., Color etching, 17.75" x 11.5"

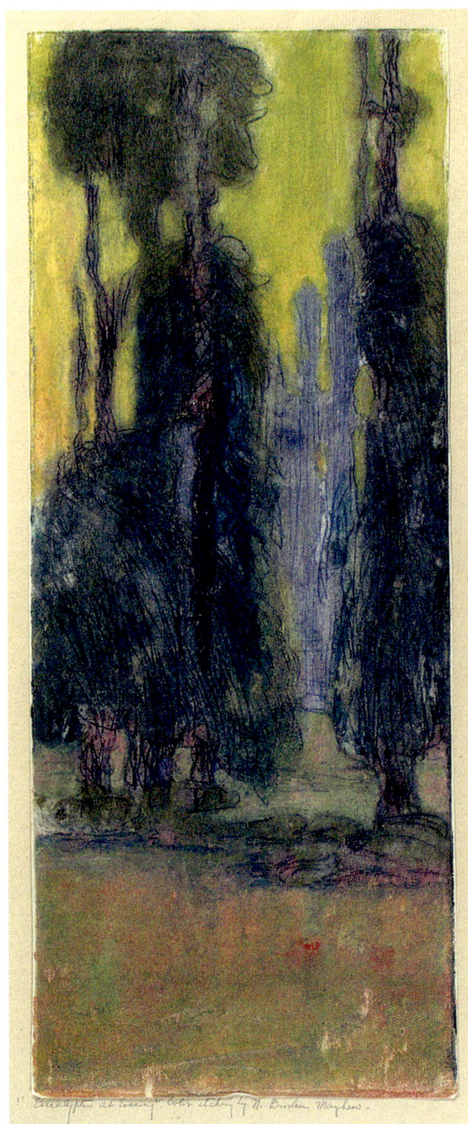

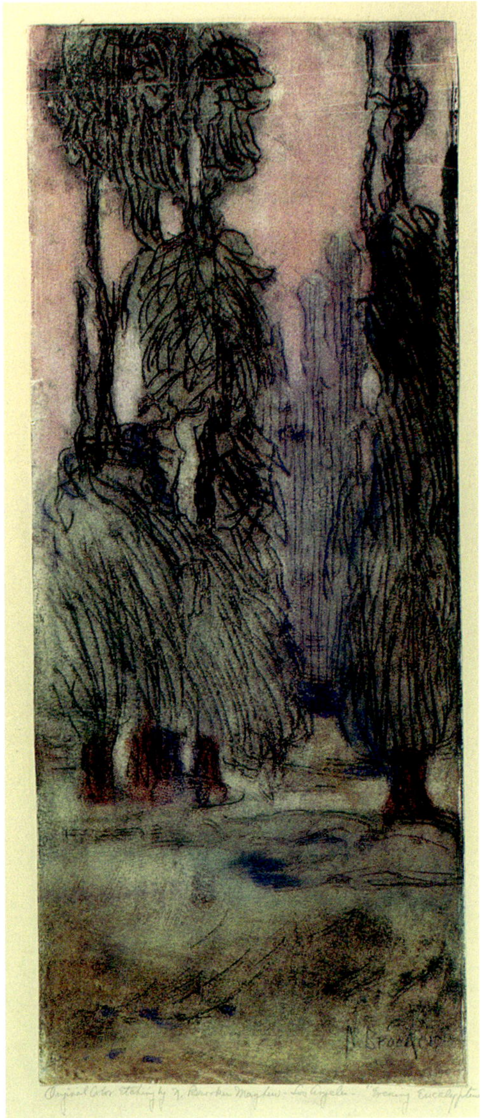

Eucalyptus at Evening
c. 1905, Color etching, 10.75" x 23.5"

Evening Eucalyptus
c. 1905, Color etching, 10.75" x 23.5"

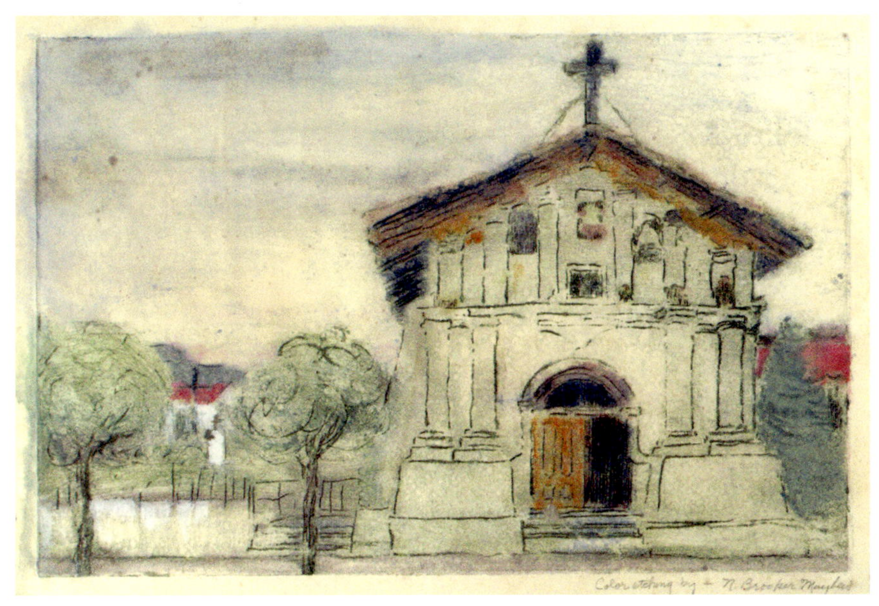

Mission Dolores
c. 1915, Color etching, 11.25" x 17"

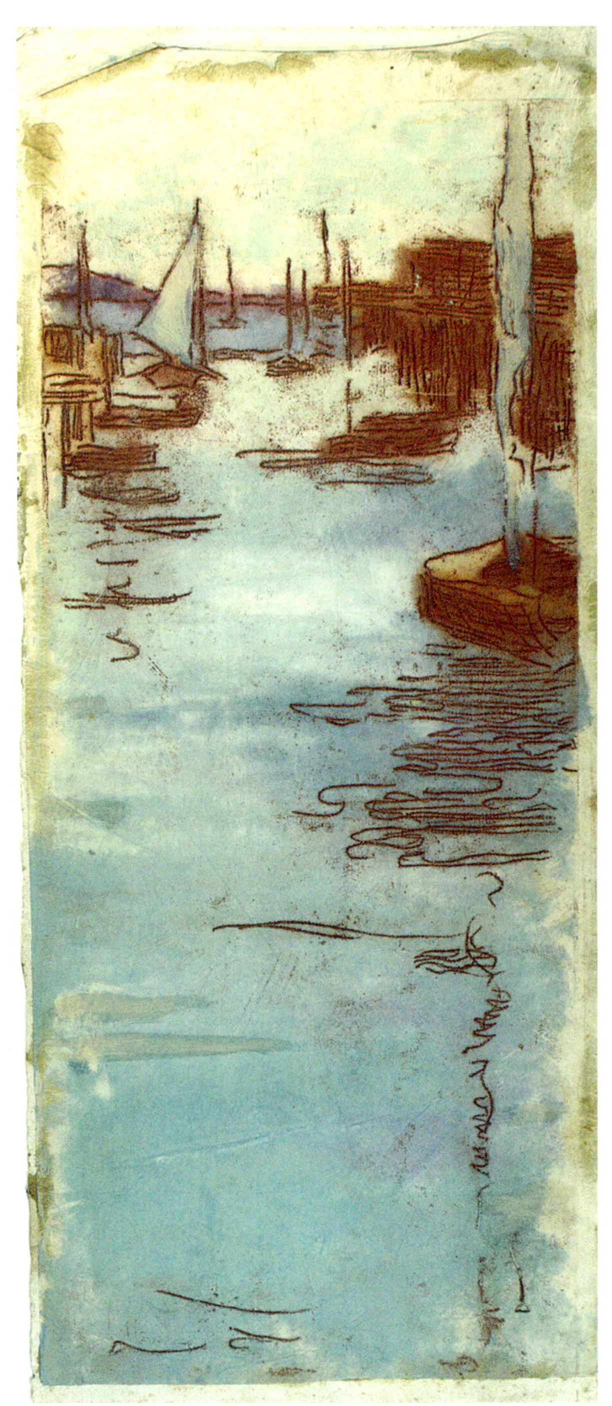

Evening Boats
c. 1905, Color etching, 19" x 8"

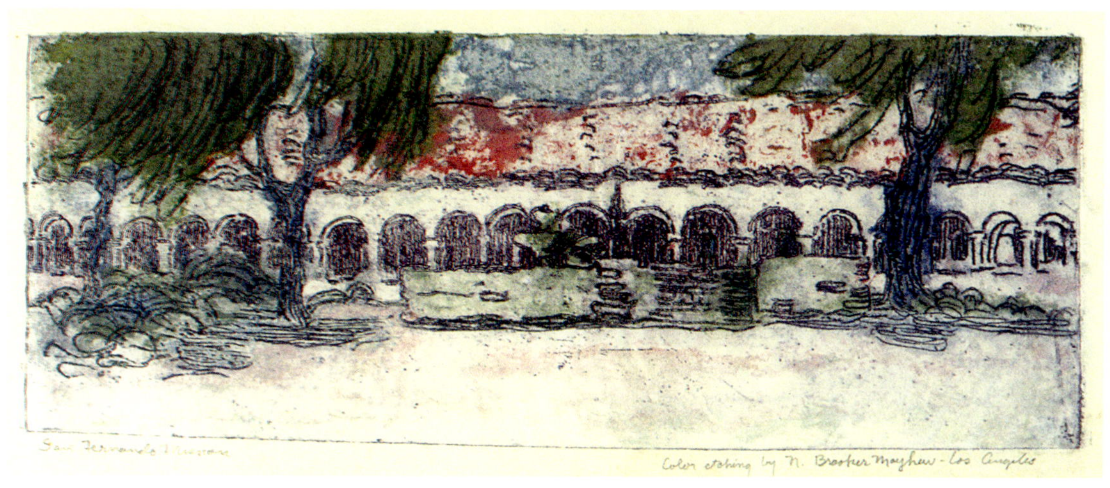

San Fernando Mission
c. 1920, Color etching, 5.5" x 15"

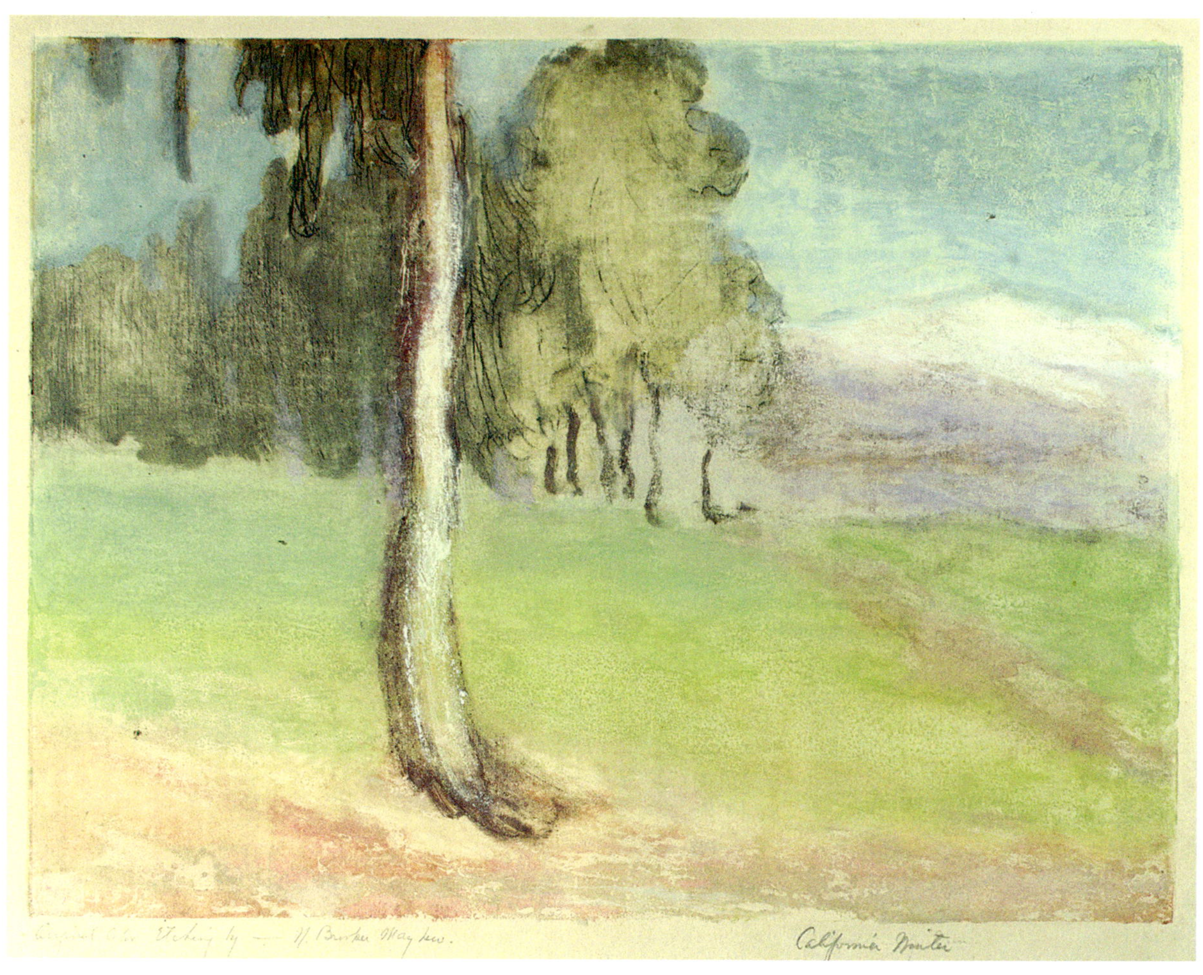

California Winter
c. 1915, Color etching, 13.75" x 18"

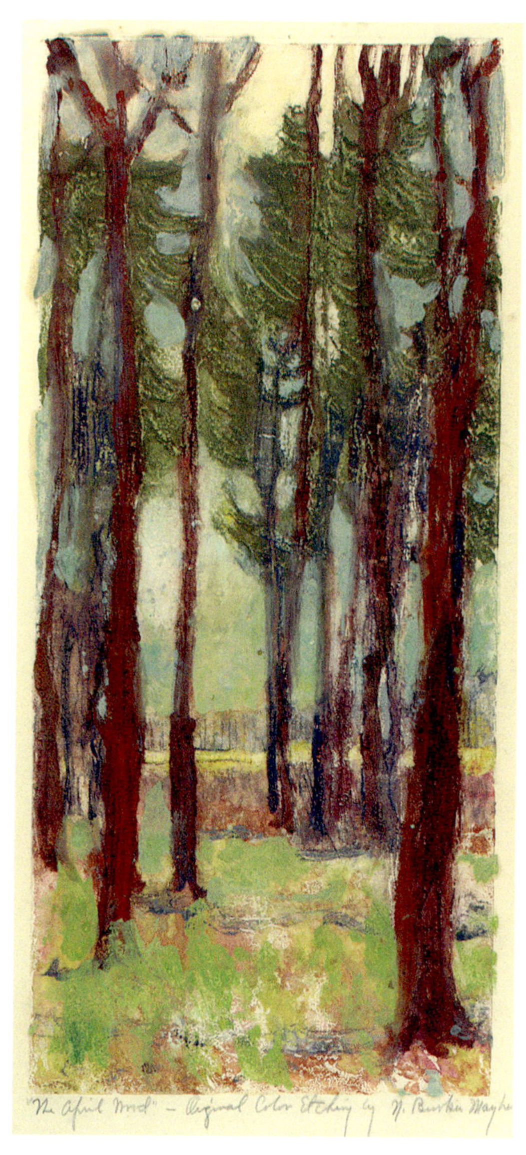

The April Wood
n.d., Color etching, 17.75" x 7.75"

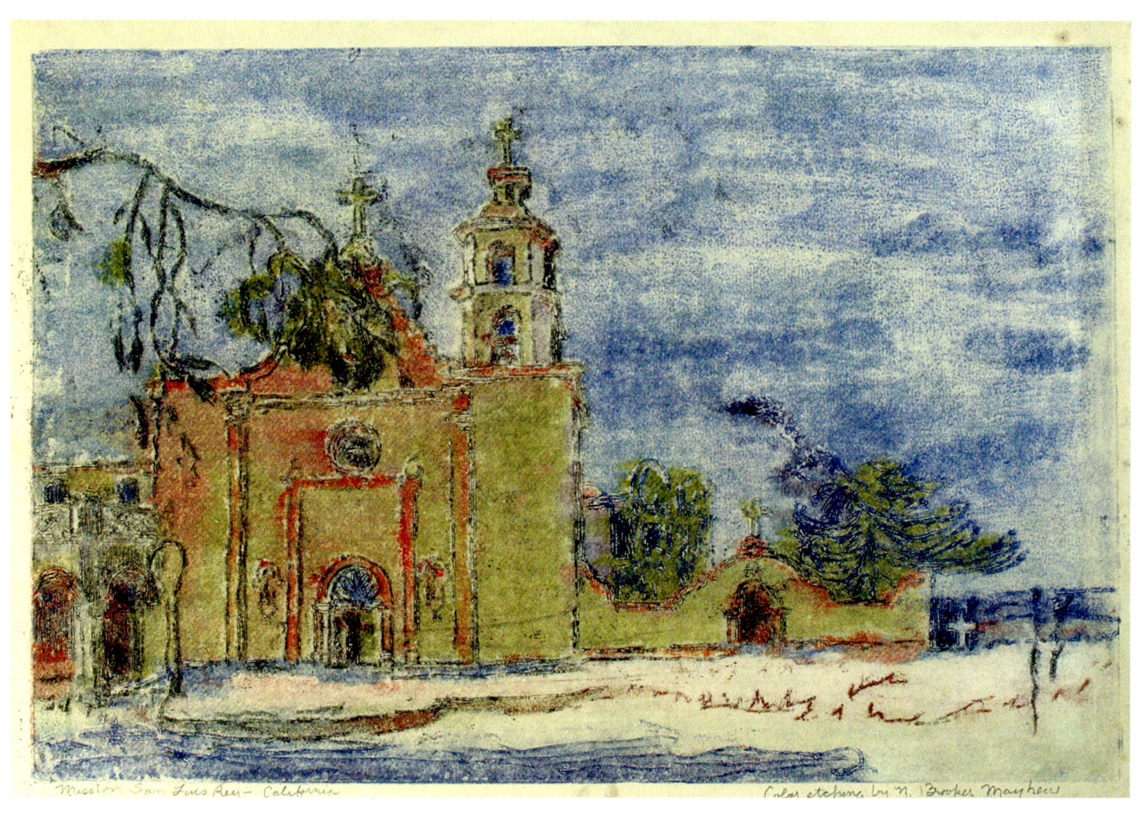

Mission San Luis Rey
c. 1914, Color etching, 11.75" x 17.25"
Collection of Marcy and Steven Morris

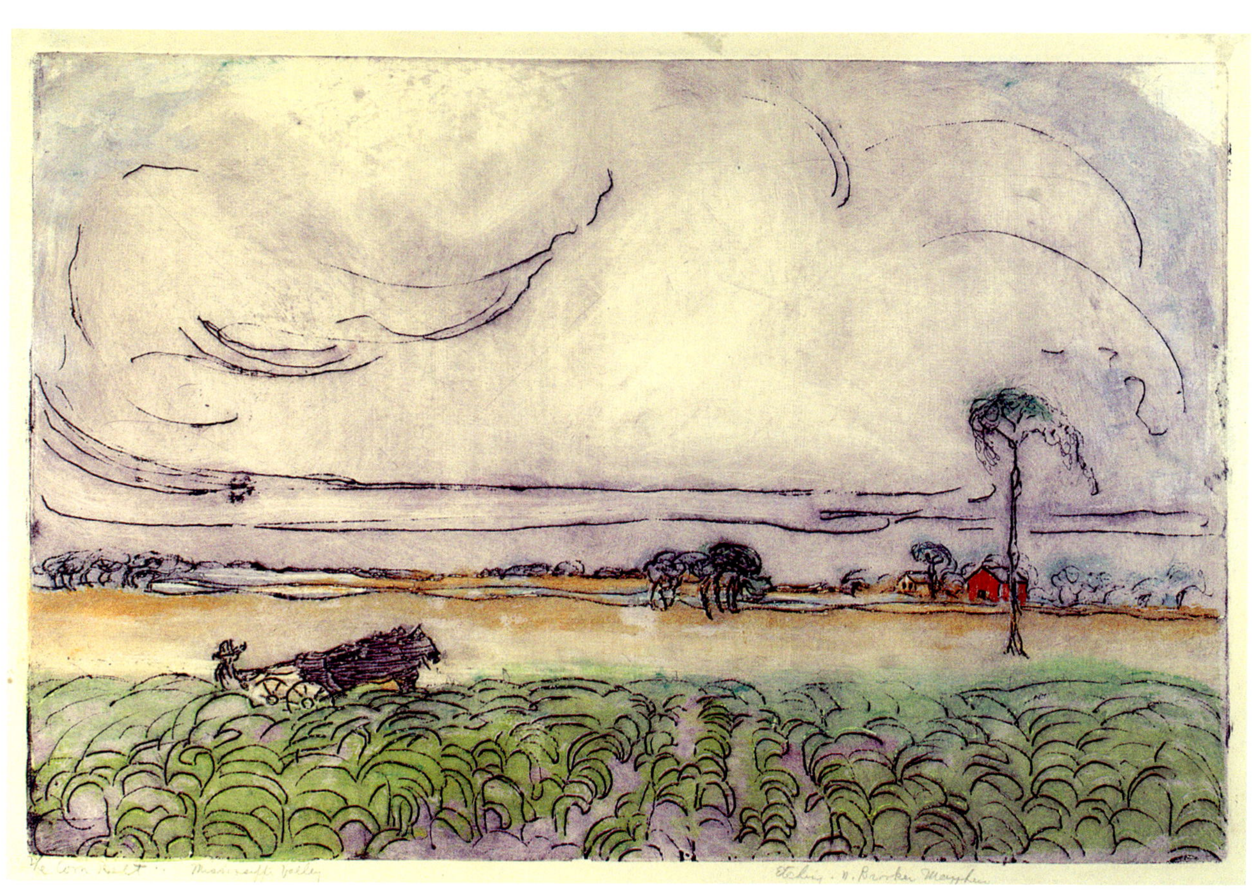

The Corn Belt
c. 1920s, Color etching, 12" x 18"

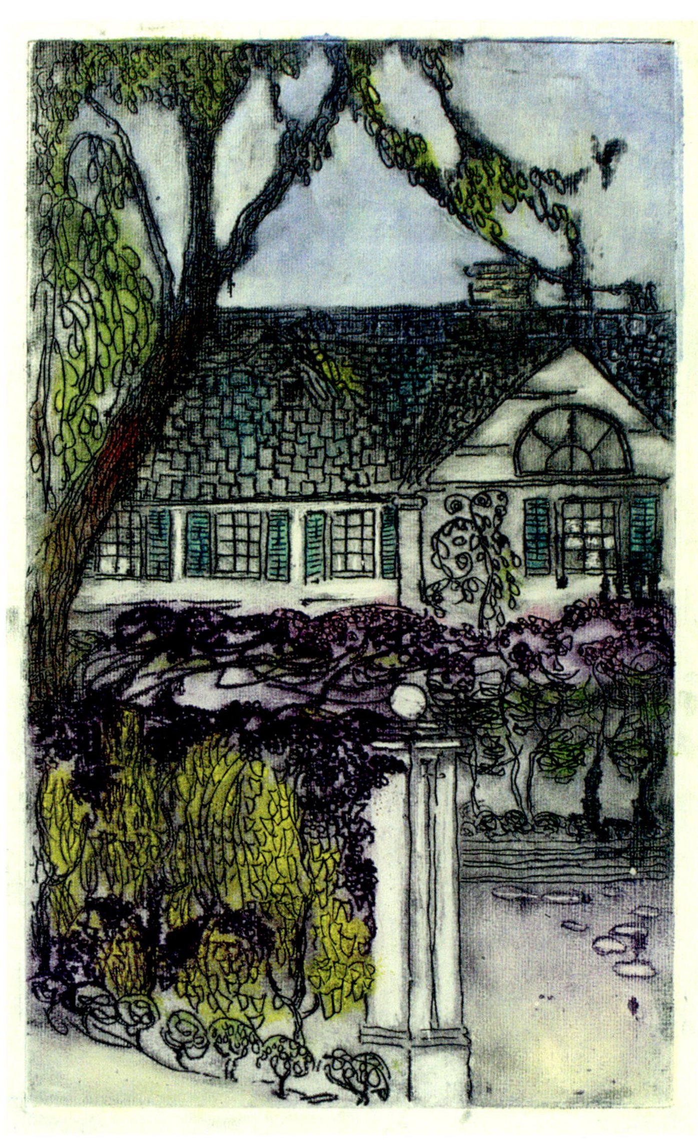

Workman's Cottage
n.d., Color etching, 14.5" x 9"

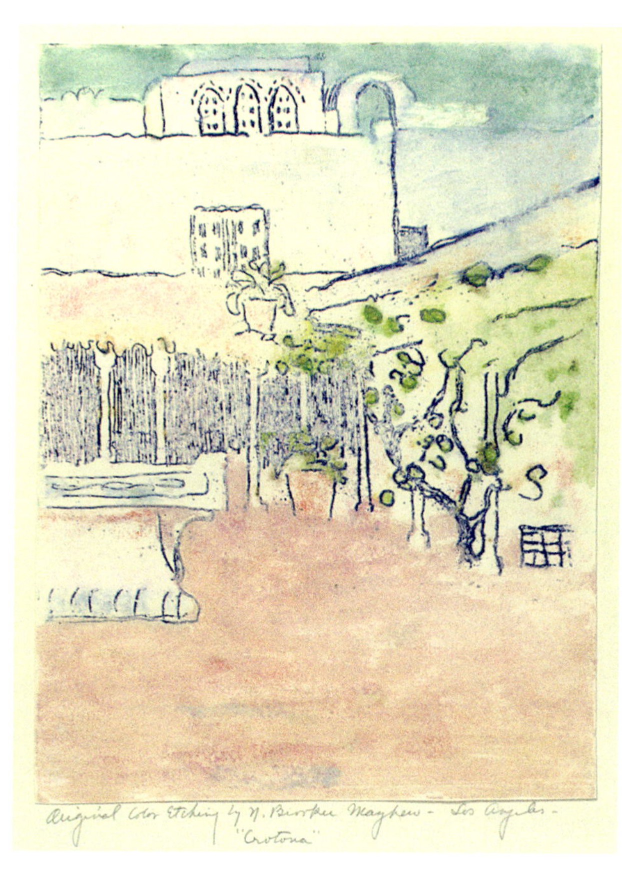

Crotona
n.d., Color etching, 9.75" x 7"

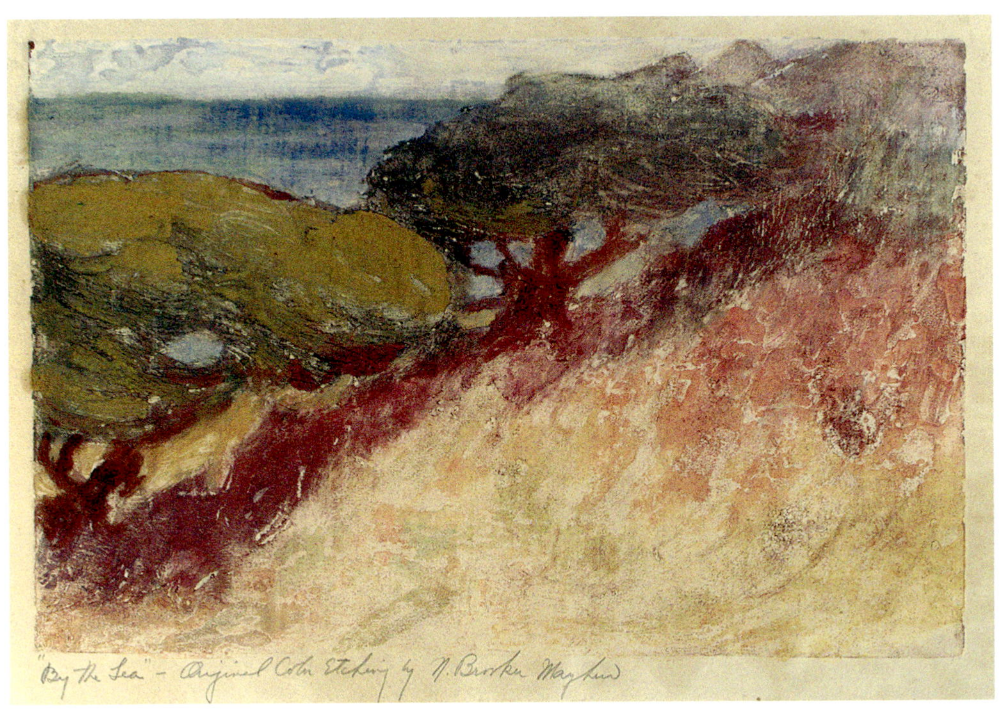

By the Sea
c. 1920s, Color etching, 9" x 13"
Collection of Tom & Lynn Meredith

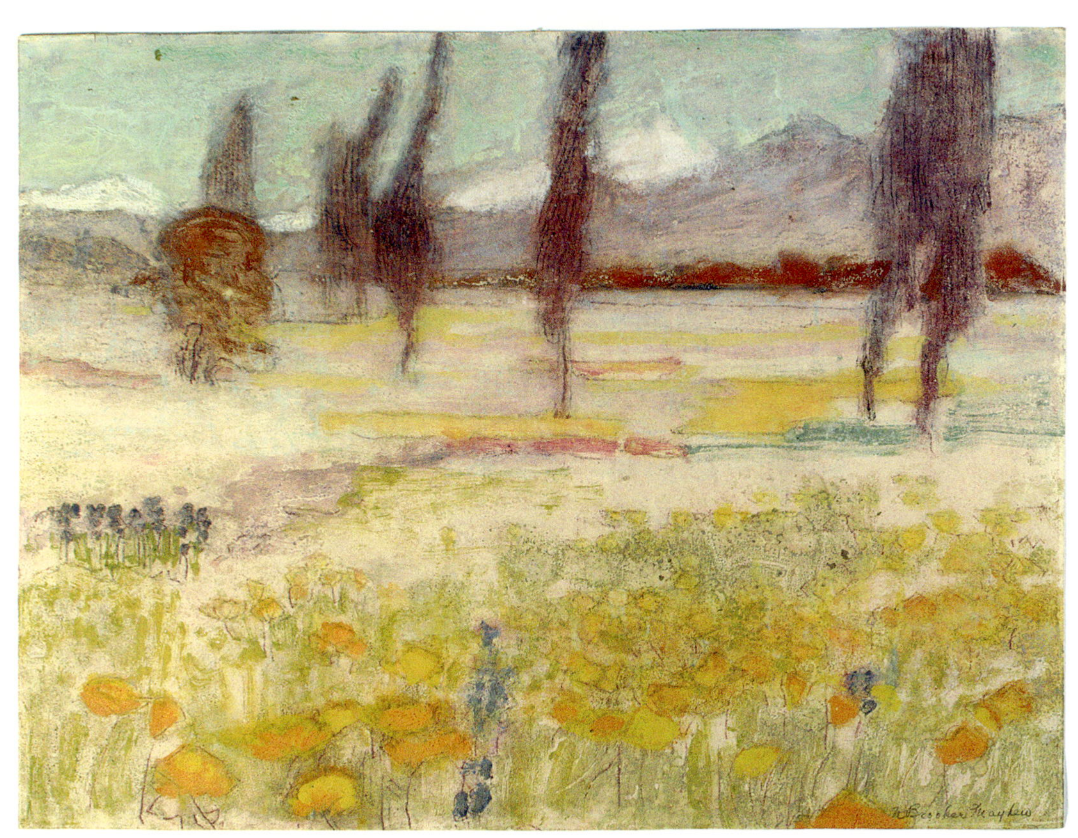

California Poppies
c. 1920, Color etching, 13.75" x 17.75"

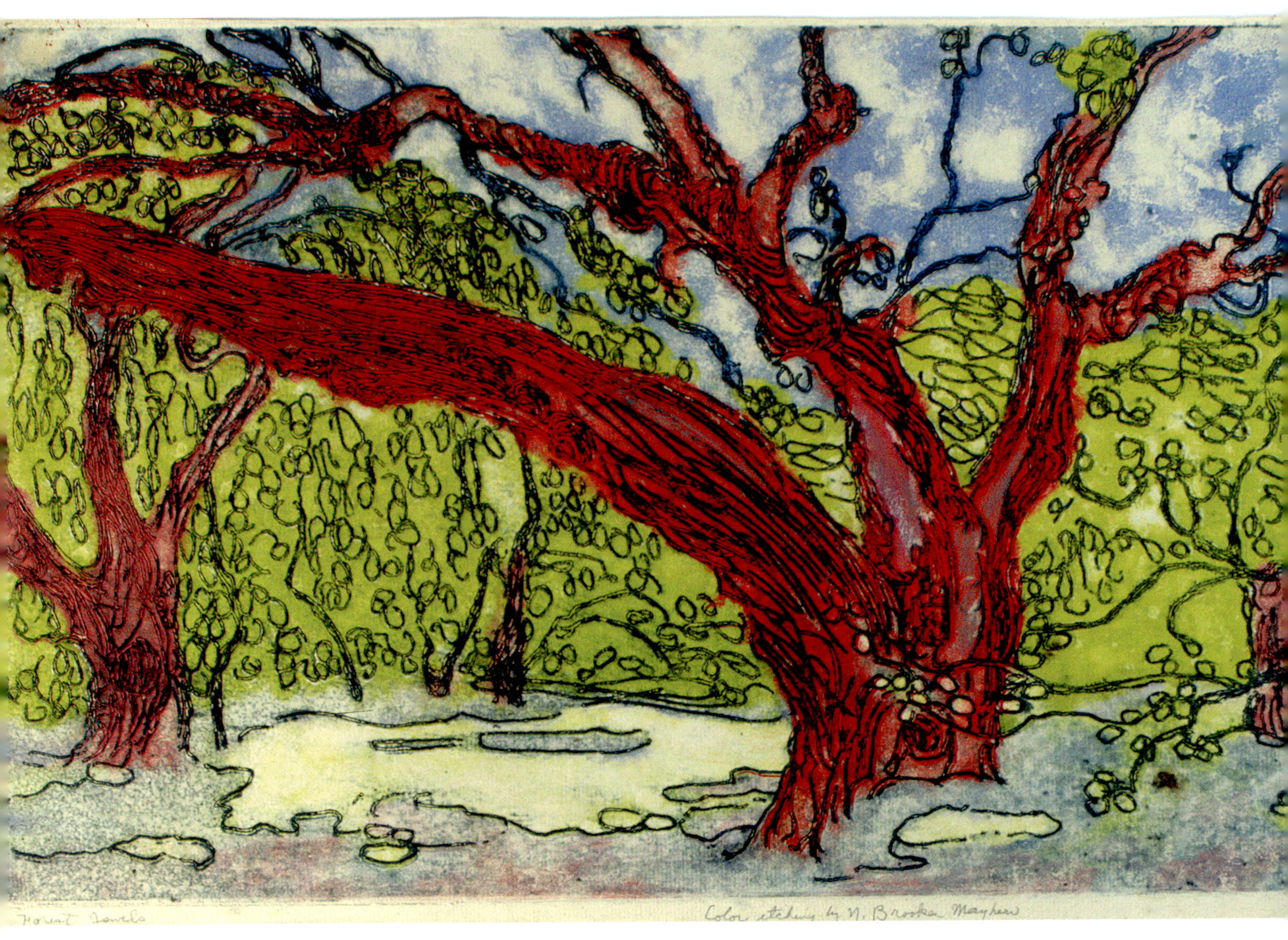

Forest Jewels
c. 1915, Color etching, 11.5" x 17"

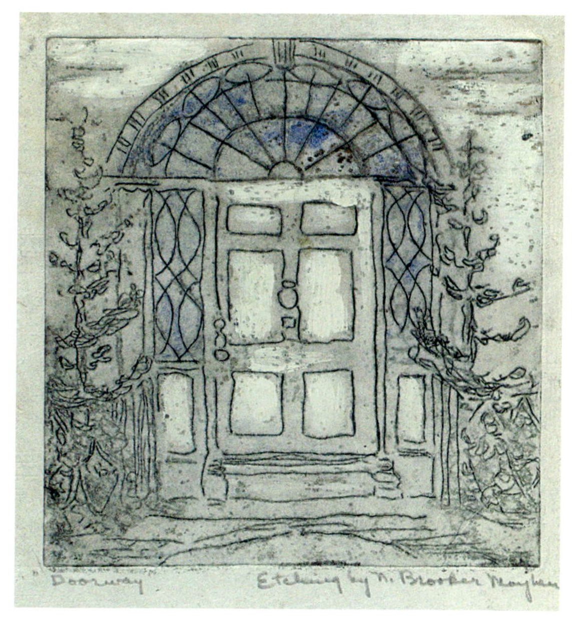

Doorway
n.d., Color ctching, 6" x 5.75"

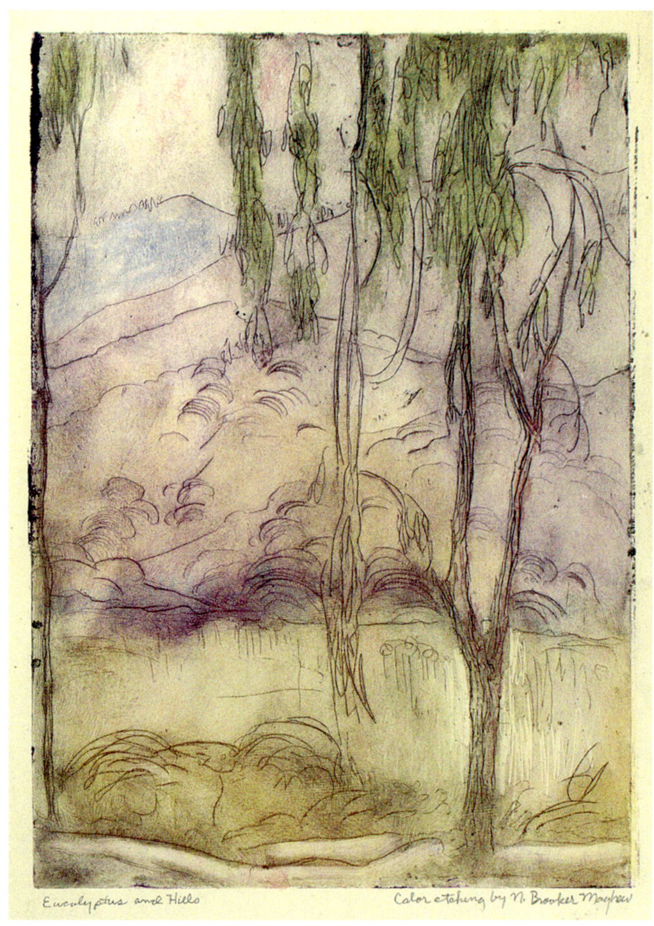

Eucalyptus and Hills
c. 1914, Color etching, 14" x 9.75"

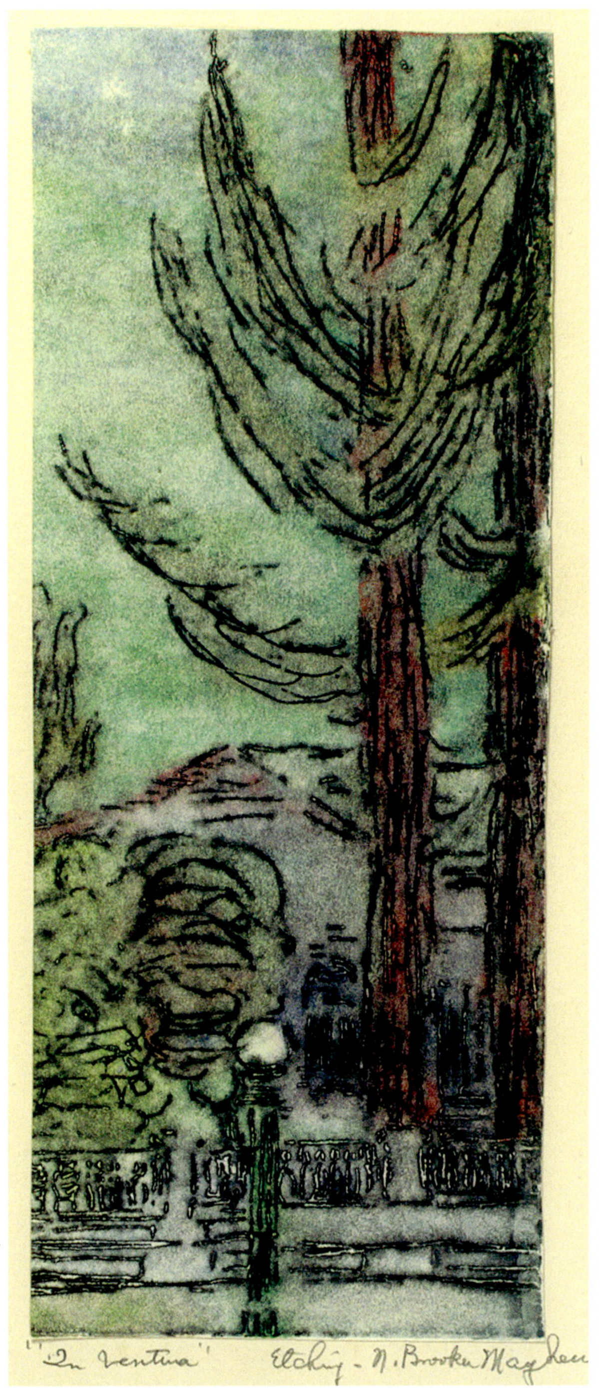

In Ventura
c. 1920s, Color etching, 12.25" x 4.75"

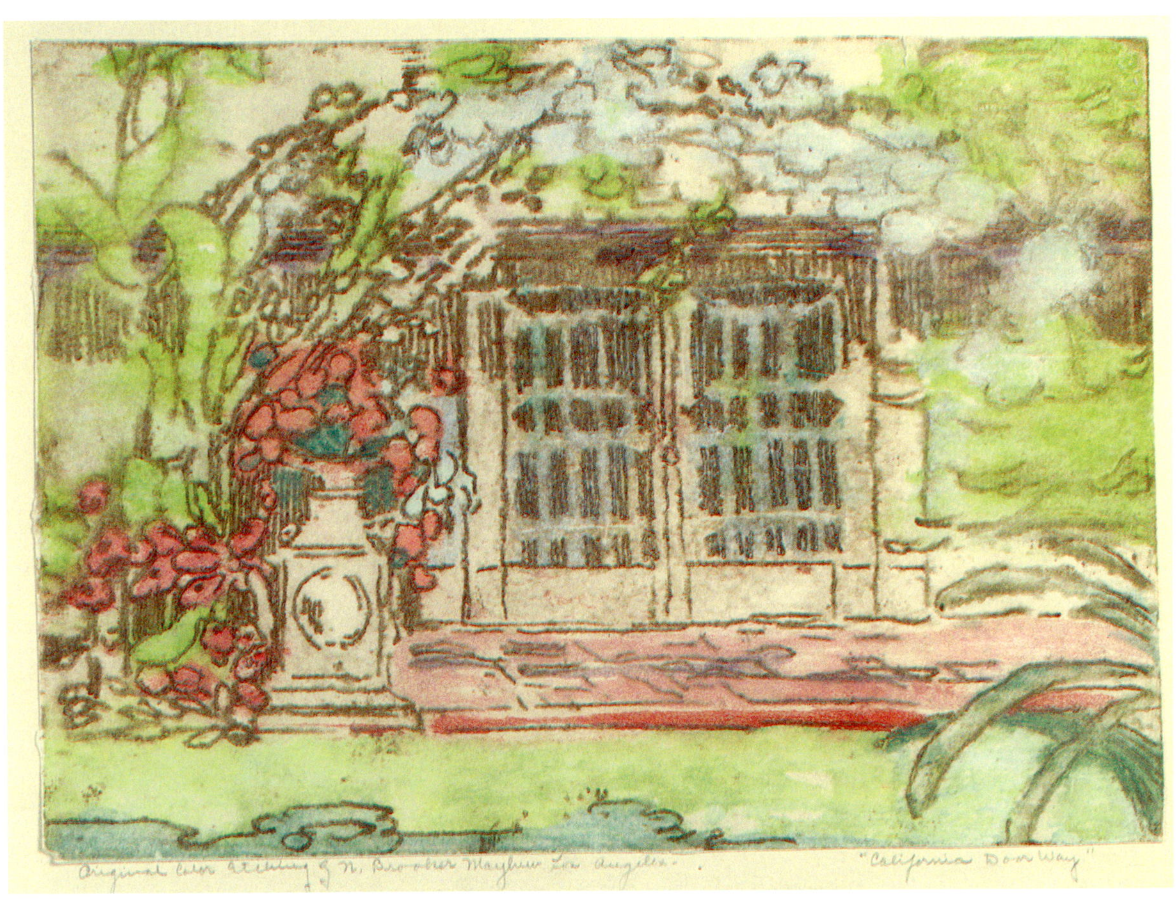

California Doorway
c. 1920s, Color etching. 9.5" x 13.25"

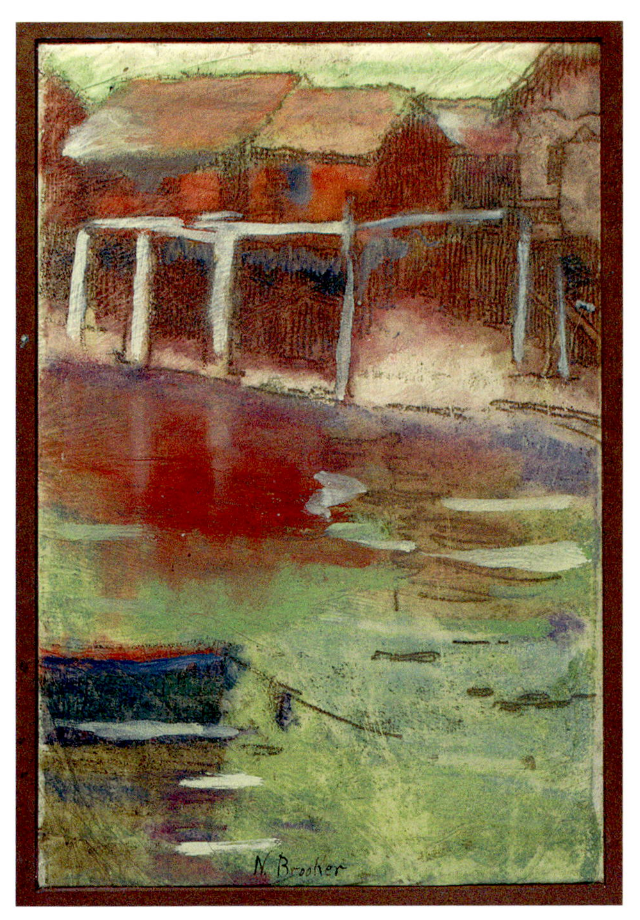

Old Wharf
c. 1910, Color etching, 12" x 7.75"

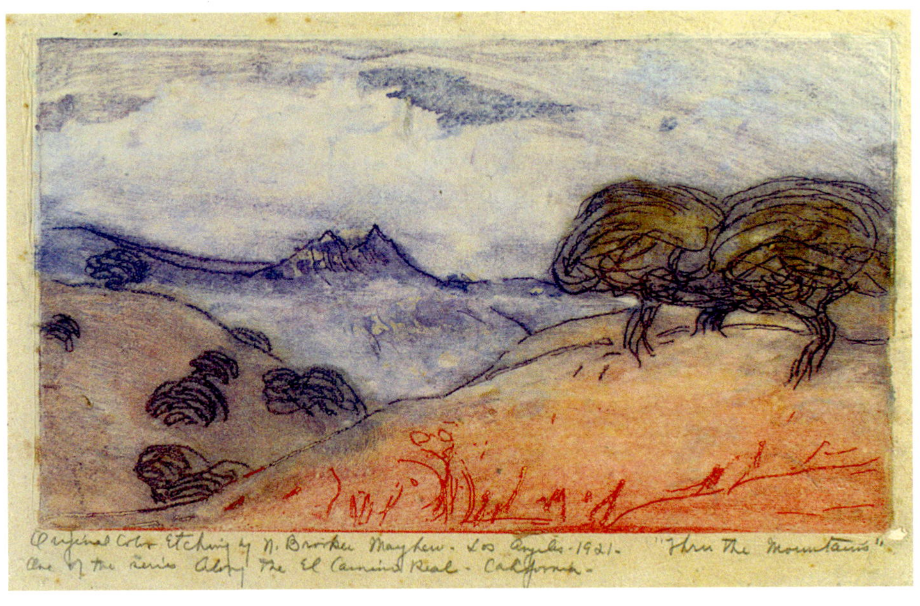

Through the Mountains
c. 1915, Color etching, 6" x 10"

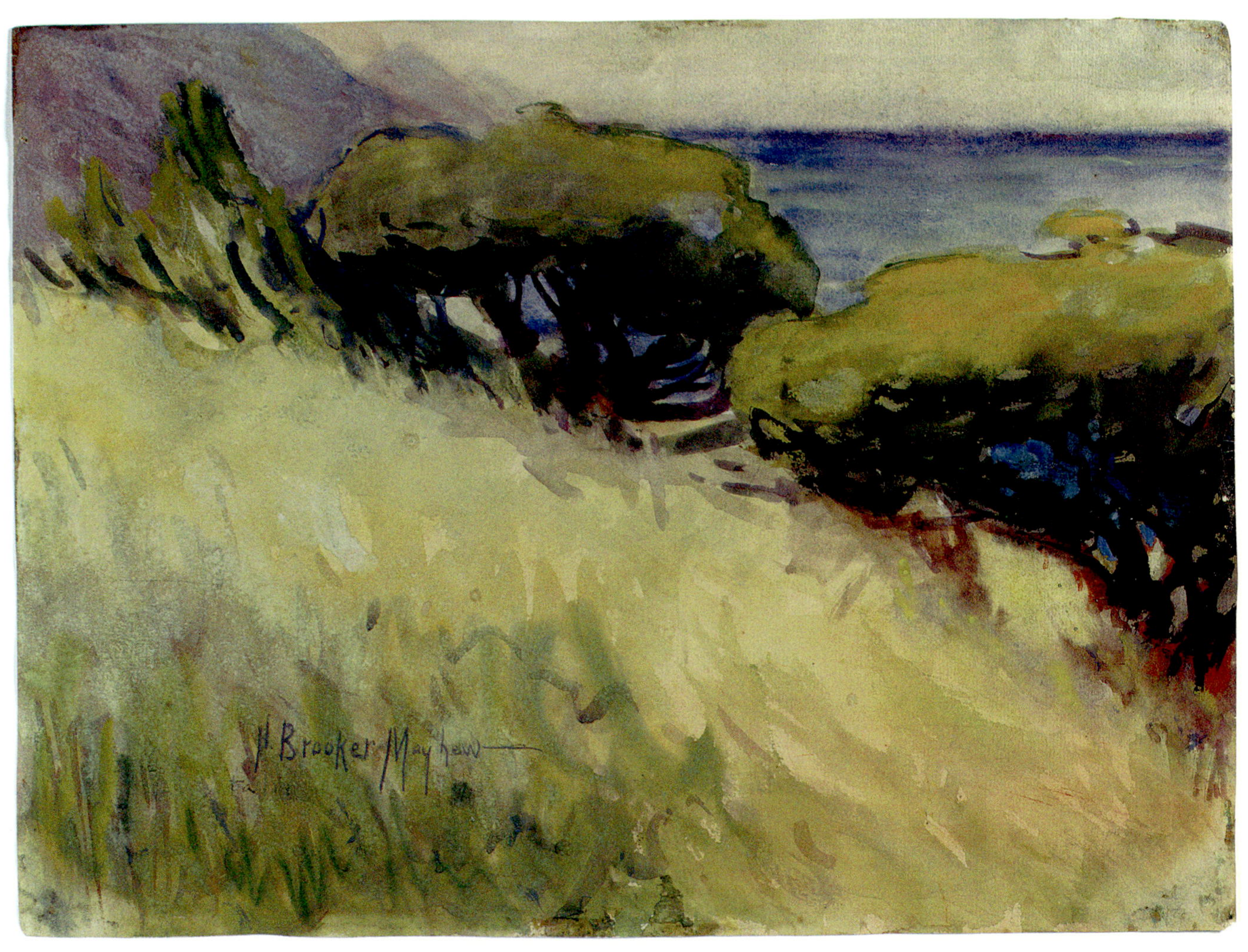

By the Sea
n.d., Watercolor, 12" x 15.75"

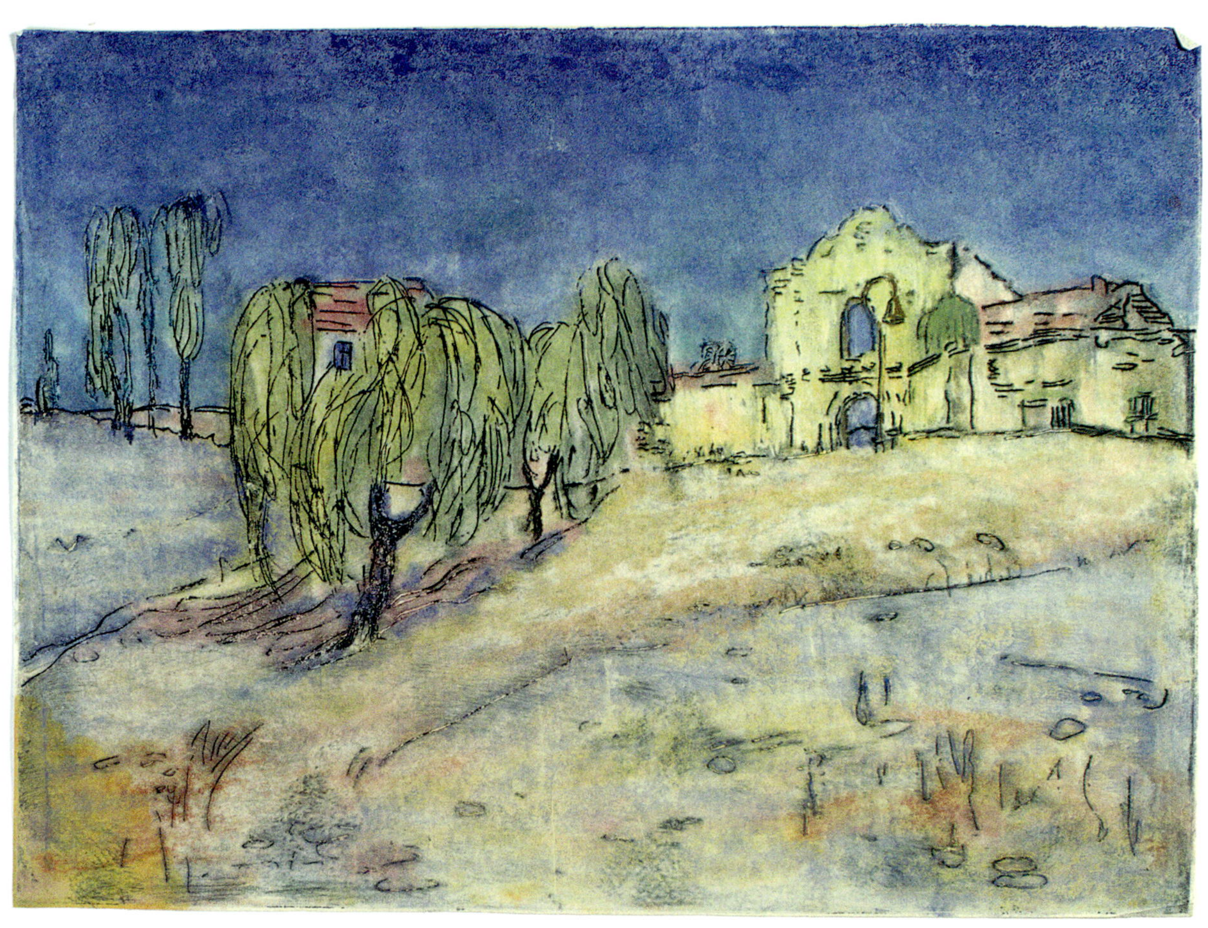

San Diego Del Alcala
c. 1920s, Color etching, 10.75" x 14.5"

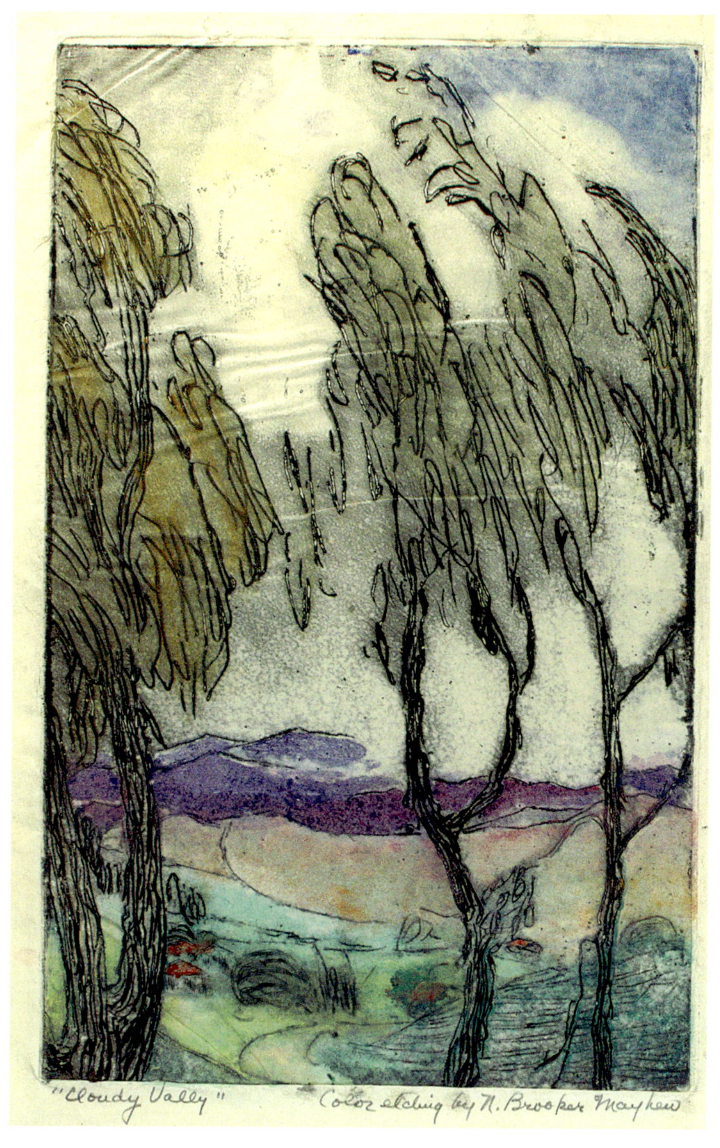

Cloudy Valley
n.d., Color etching, 12.5" x 8"

Untitled, Symbolist Adobe
c. 1910, Color etching, 11.75" x 8"

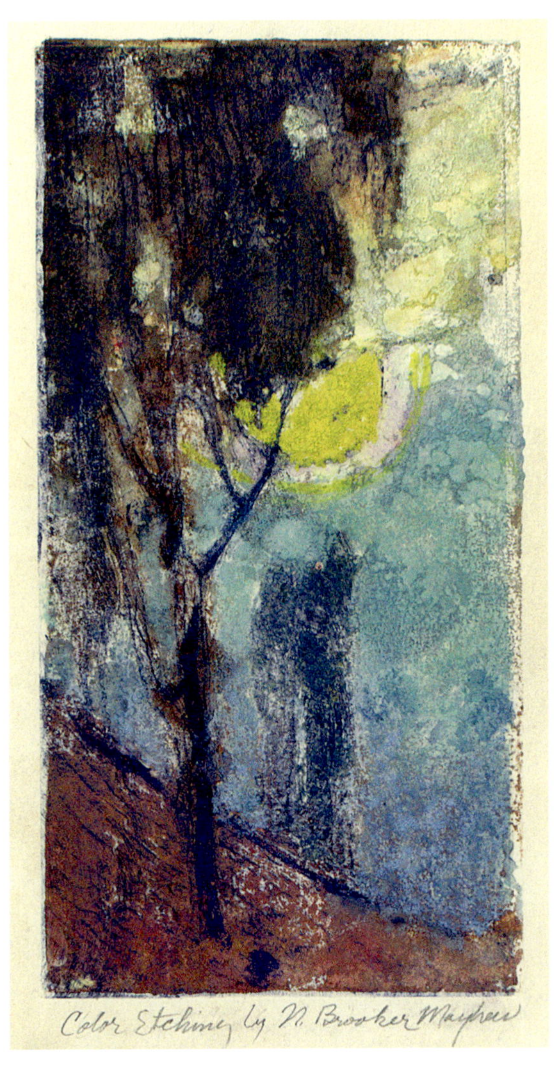

In the Gloaming
n.d., Color etching, 8" x 4"

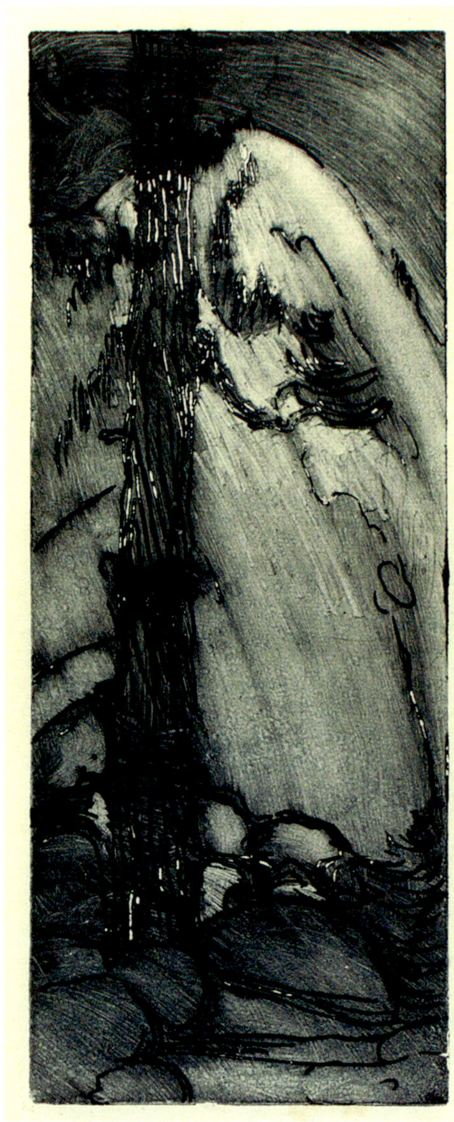

Untitled, A Tree at Night
n.d., Color etching, 11" x 4.25"

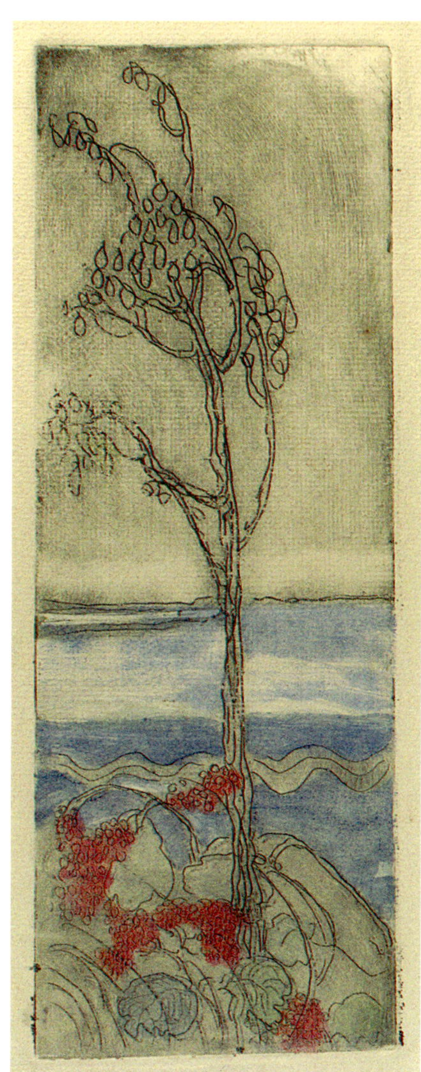

Untitled, A Tree by Day
n.d., Color etching, 10.75" x 3.75"

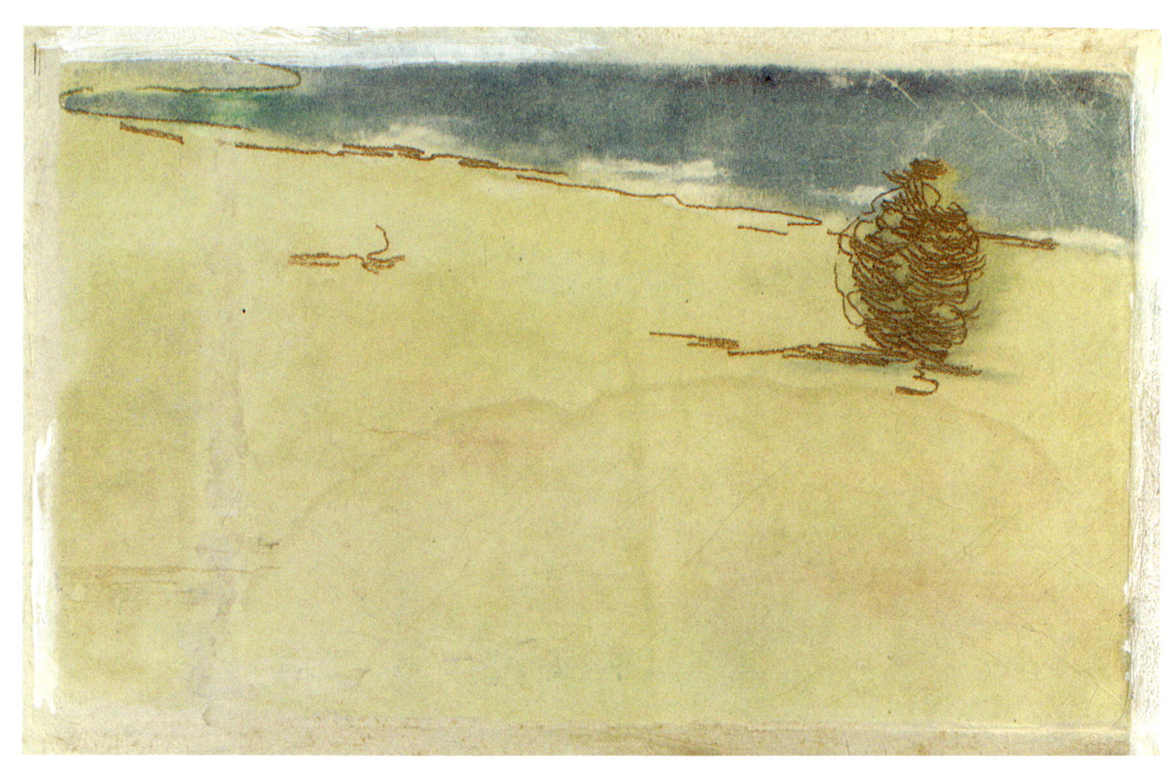

Untitled, A Lone Scrub Brush
c. 1915, Color etching, 7.5" x 11.75"

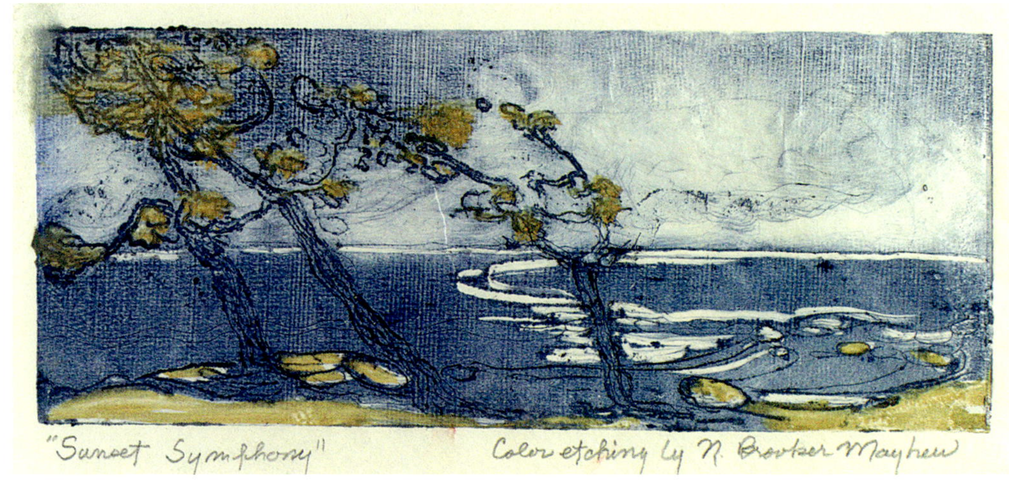

Sunset Symphony
c. 1910, Color etching, 3.25" x 9"

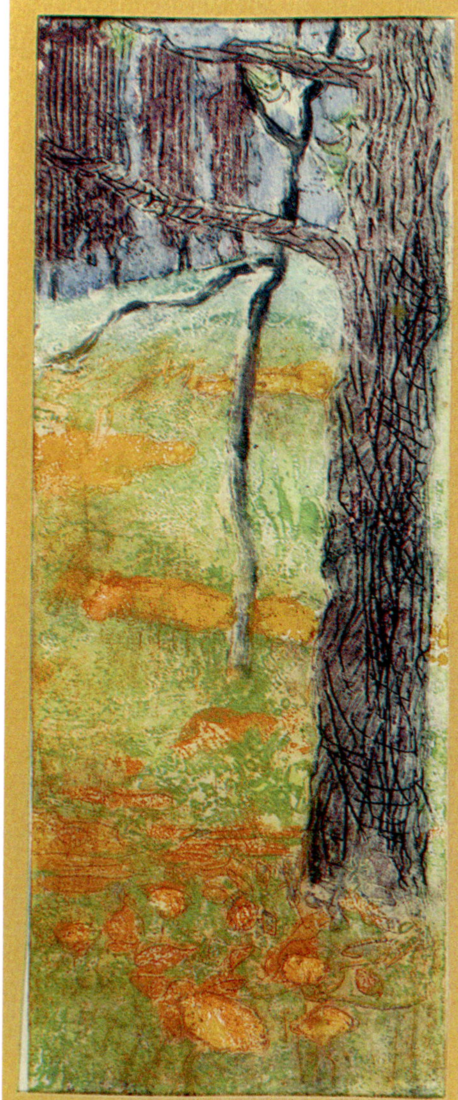

Pleasant Places
1912, Color etching, 7.75" x 3"

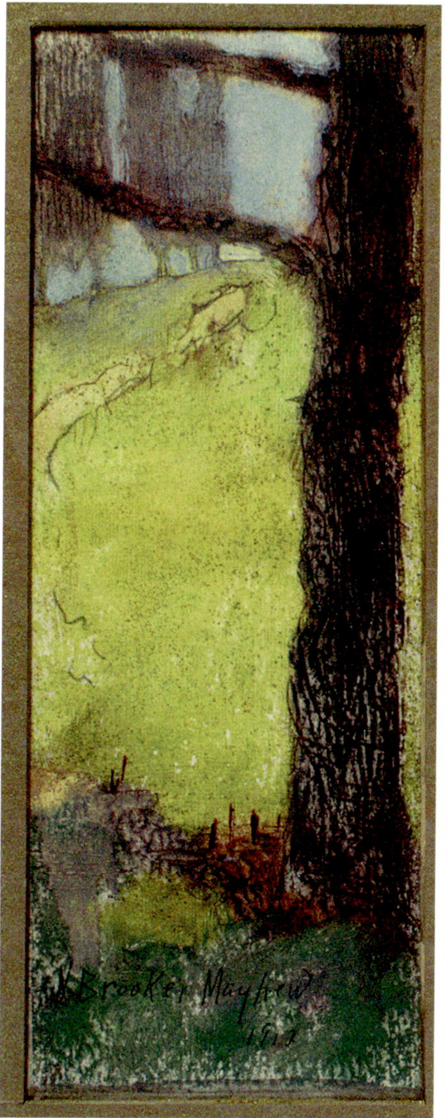

Pleasant Places
1912, Color etching, 7.75" x 3"
Collection of Sullivan Goss — An American Gallery

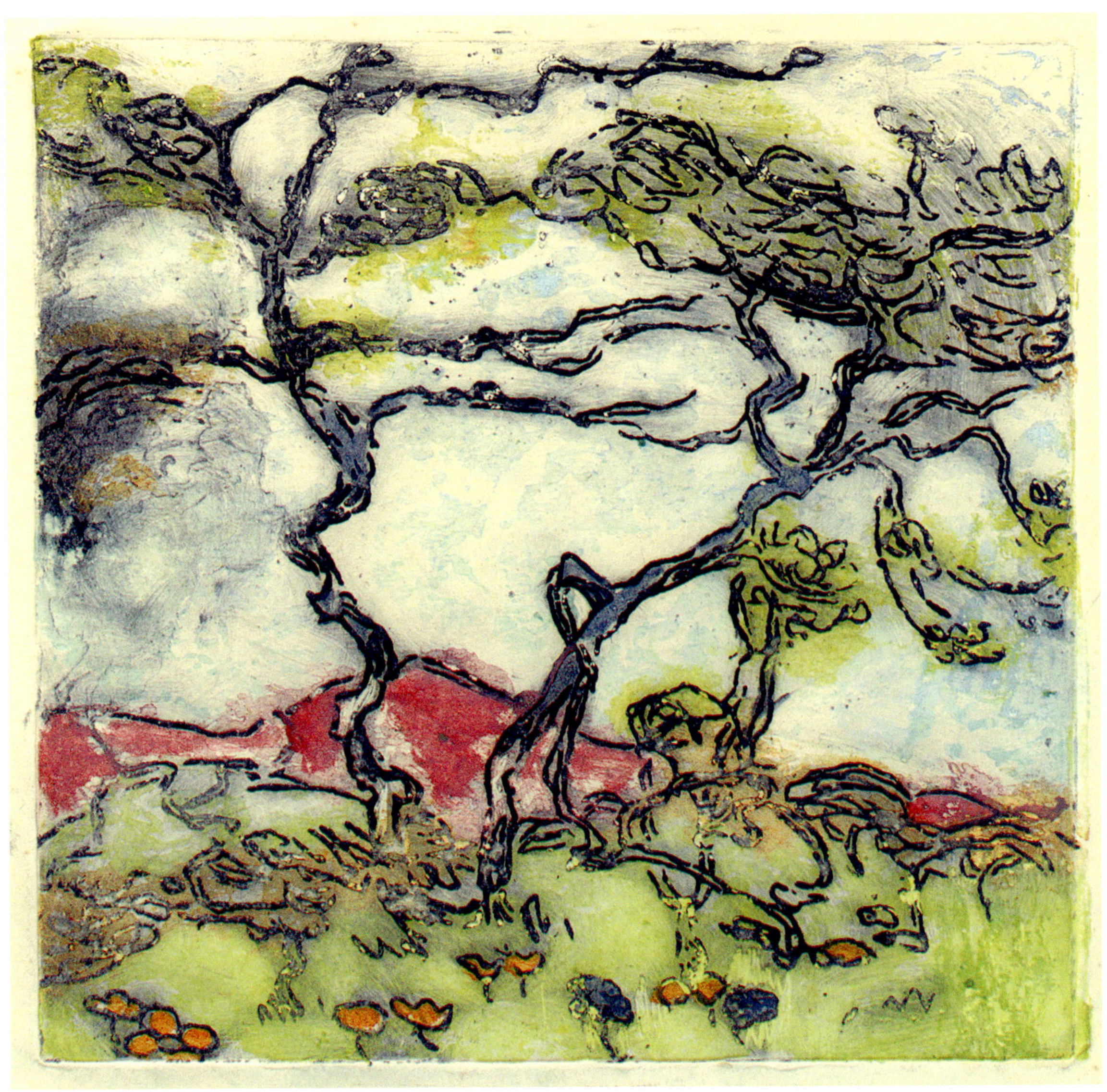

Song of the Sycamores
c. 1910, Color etching, 7.75" x 7.5"

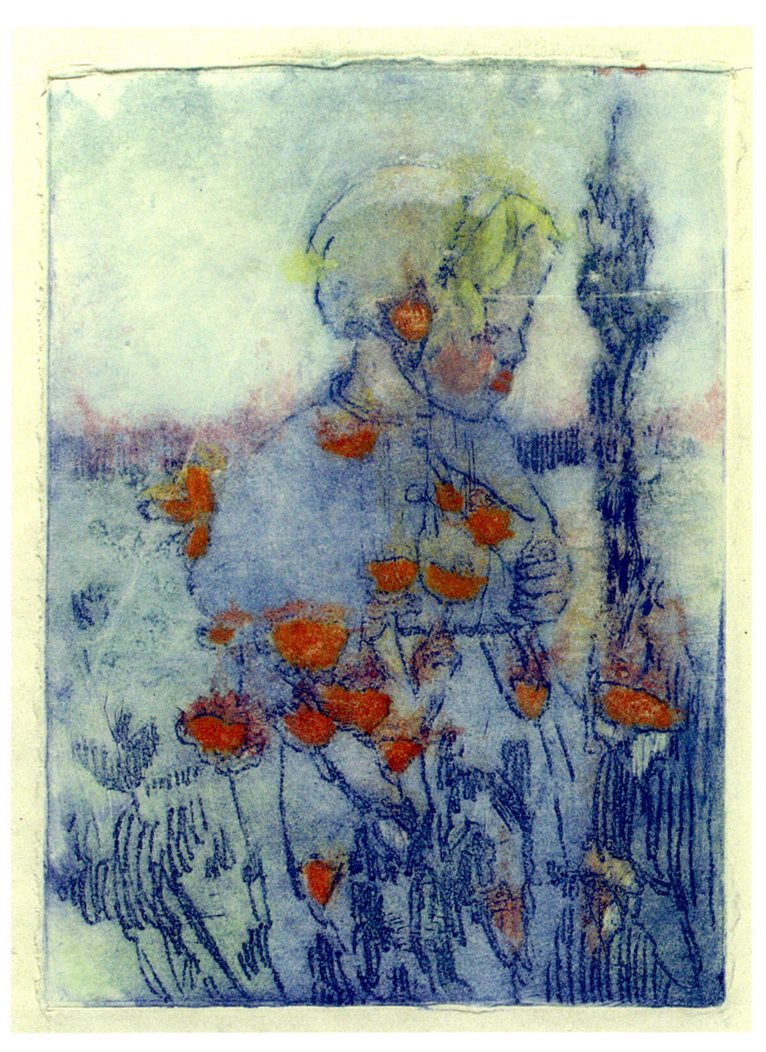

Child
n.d., Color etching, 7" x 5"

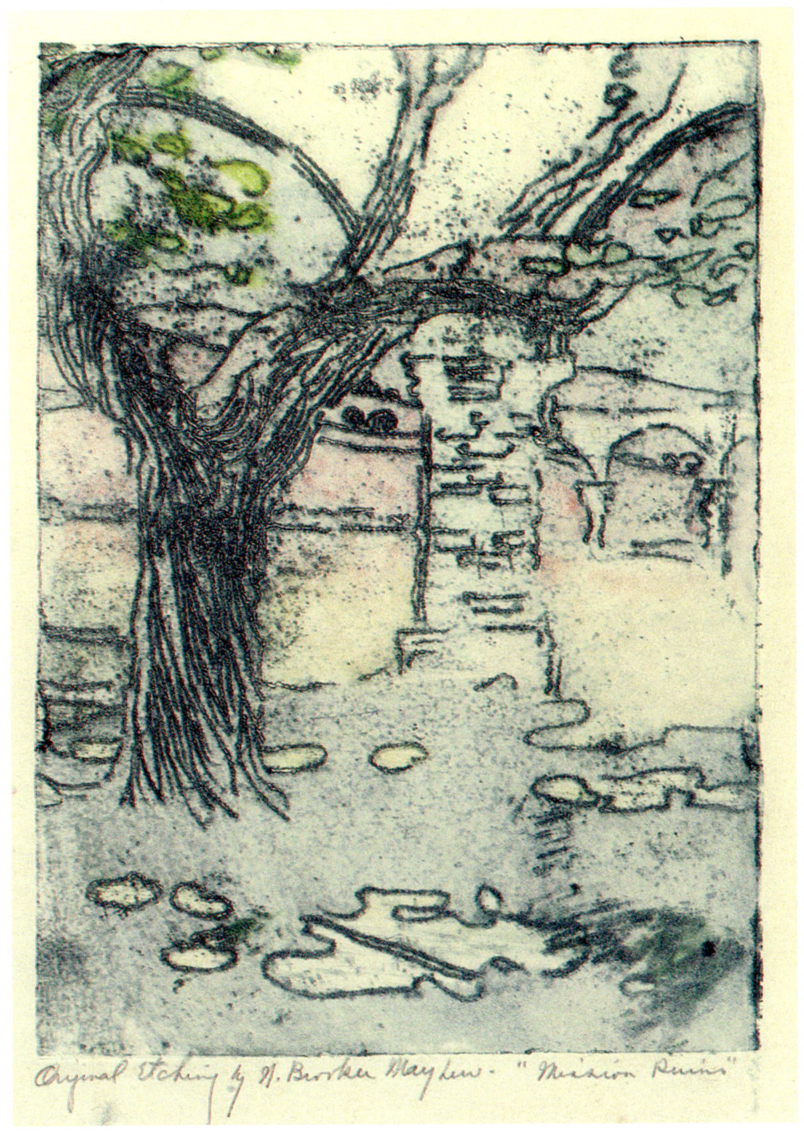

Mission Ruins
c. 1920, Color etching, 9.75" x 7"

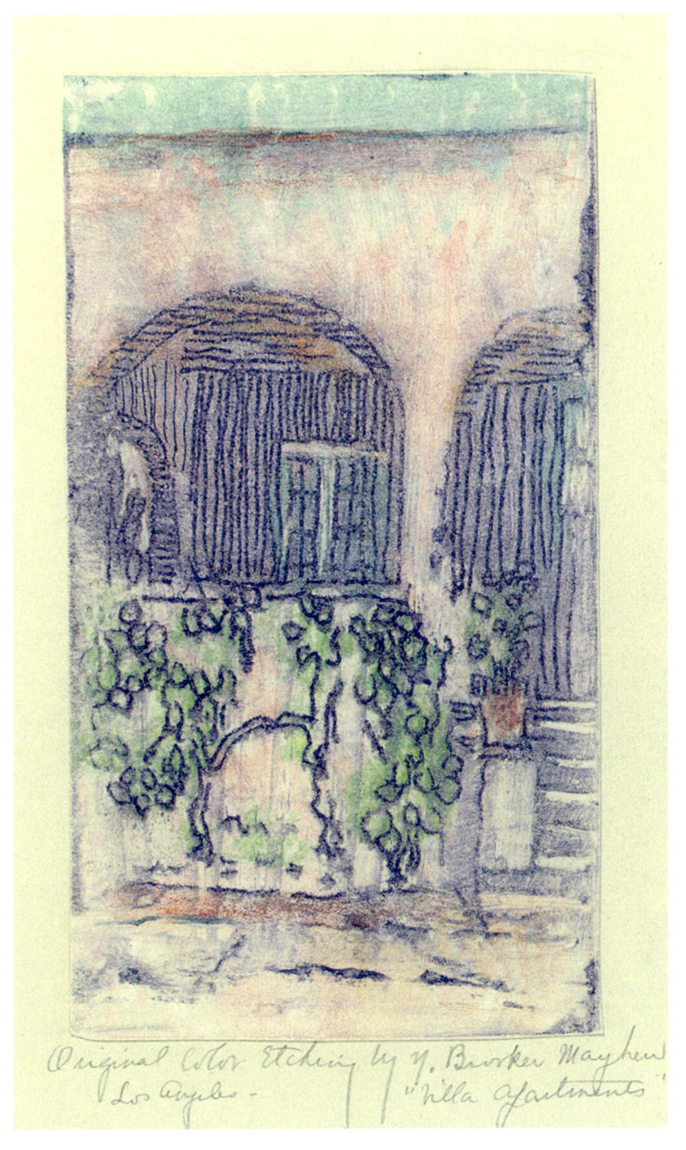

Villa Apartments
c. 1920s, Color etching, 7" x 3.75"

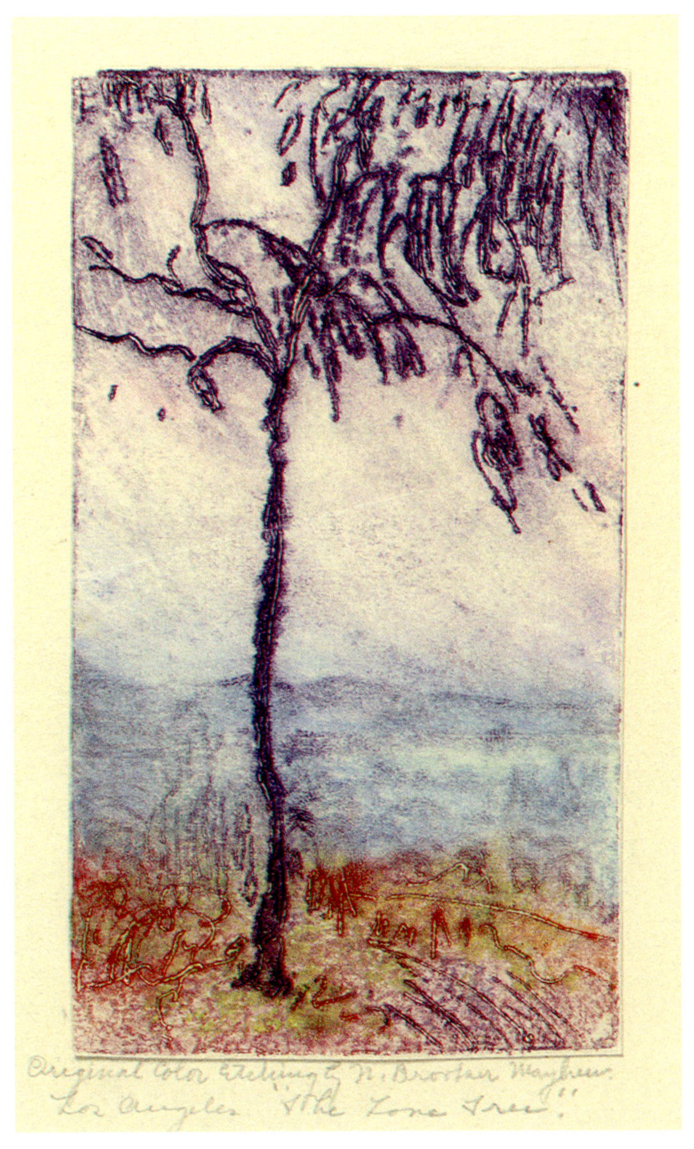

The Lone Tree
c. 1910, Color etching, 6.75" x 3.75"

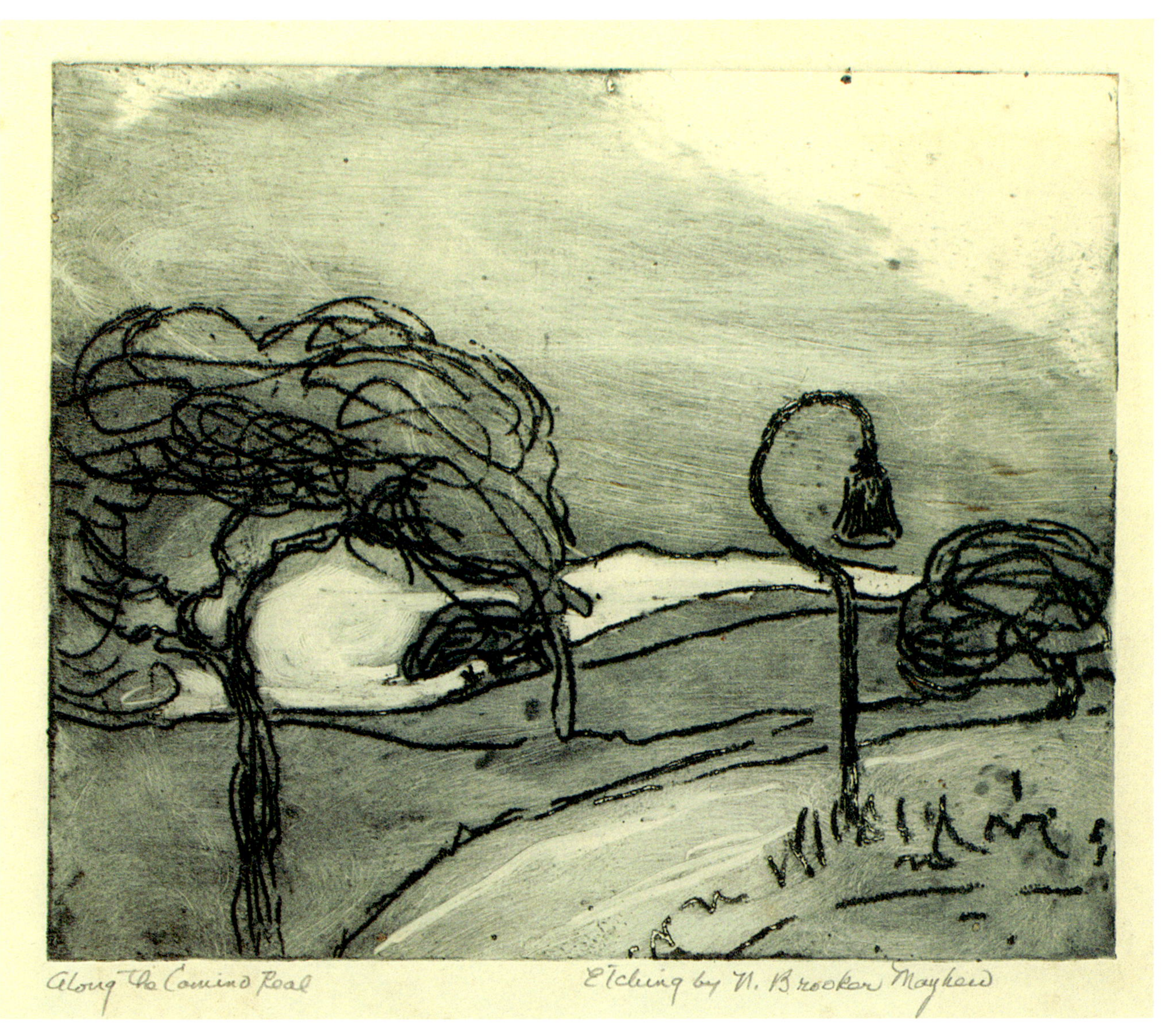

Along the Camino Real
c. 1915, Color etching, 6.5" x 7.75"

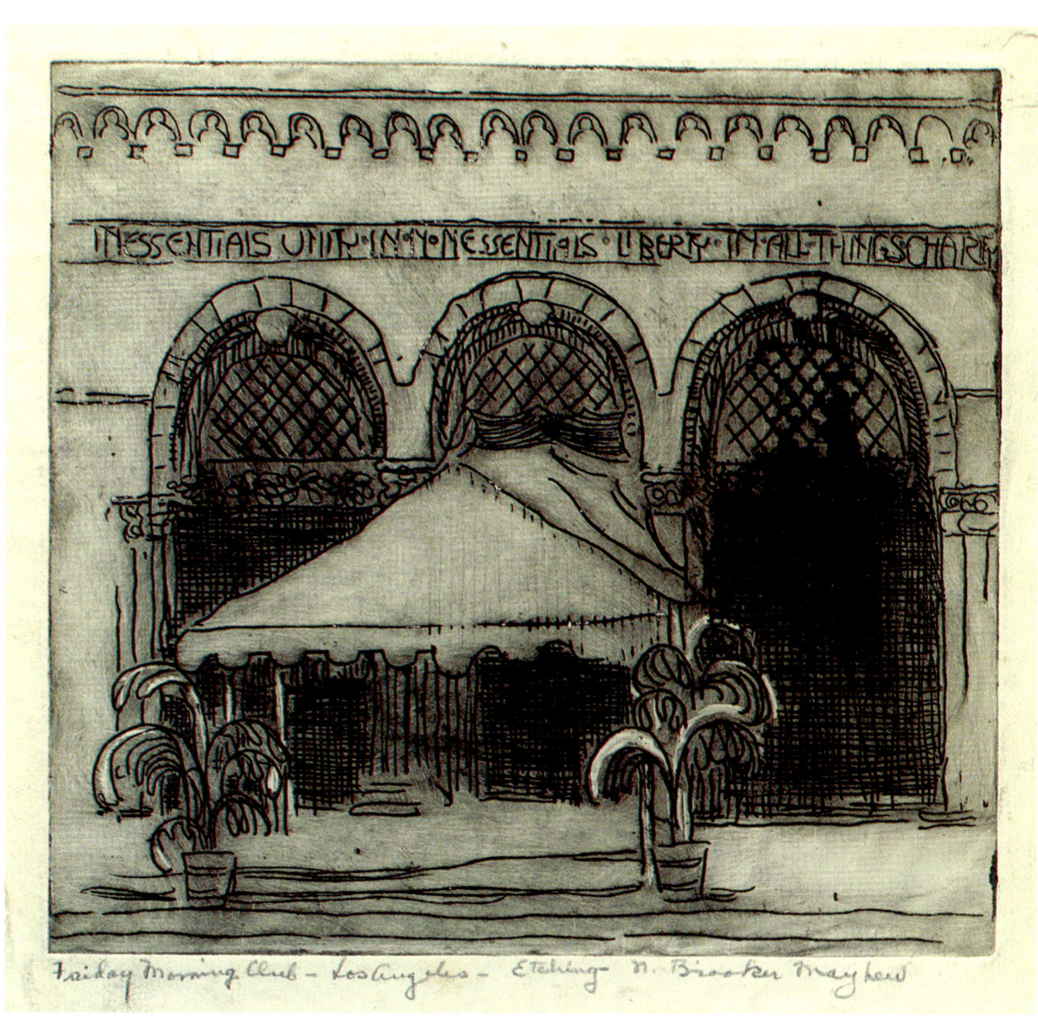

Friday Morning Club
c. 1920s, Color etching, 6.75" x 7"

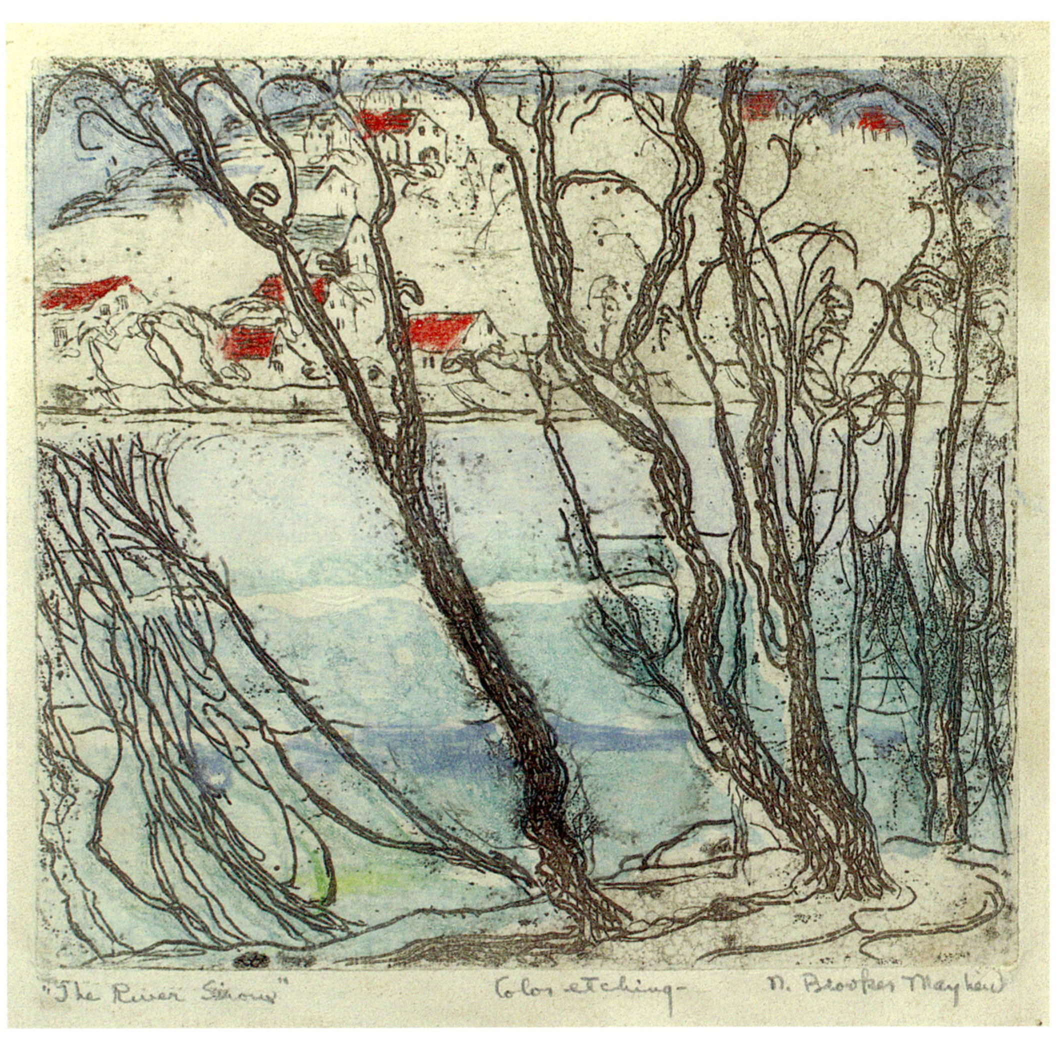

The River Sioux
n.d., Color etching, 7.5" x 8.25"

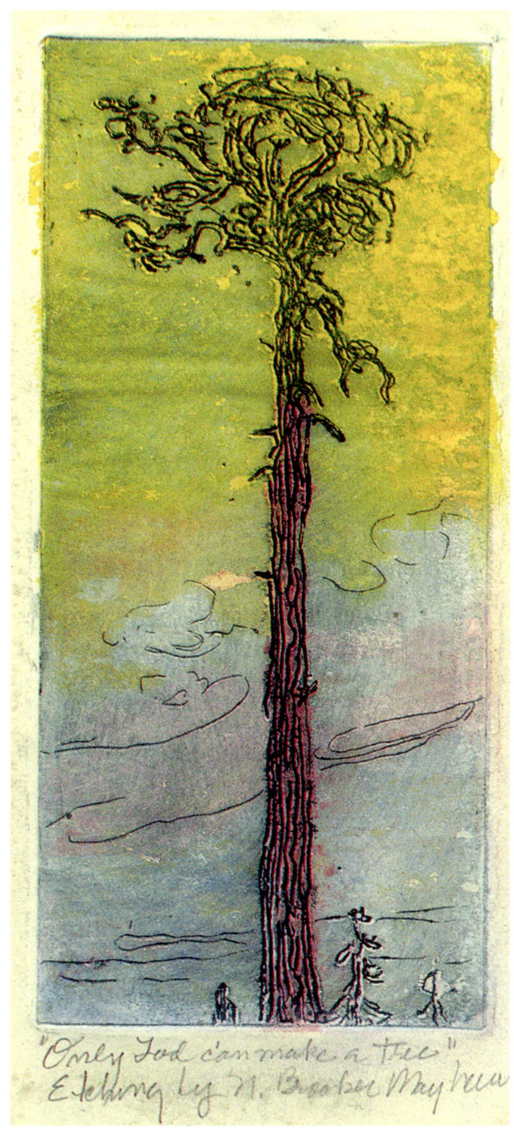

Only God Can Make a Tree
c. 1905, Color etching, 8.75" x 4"

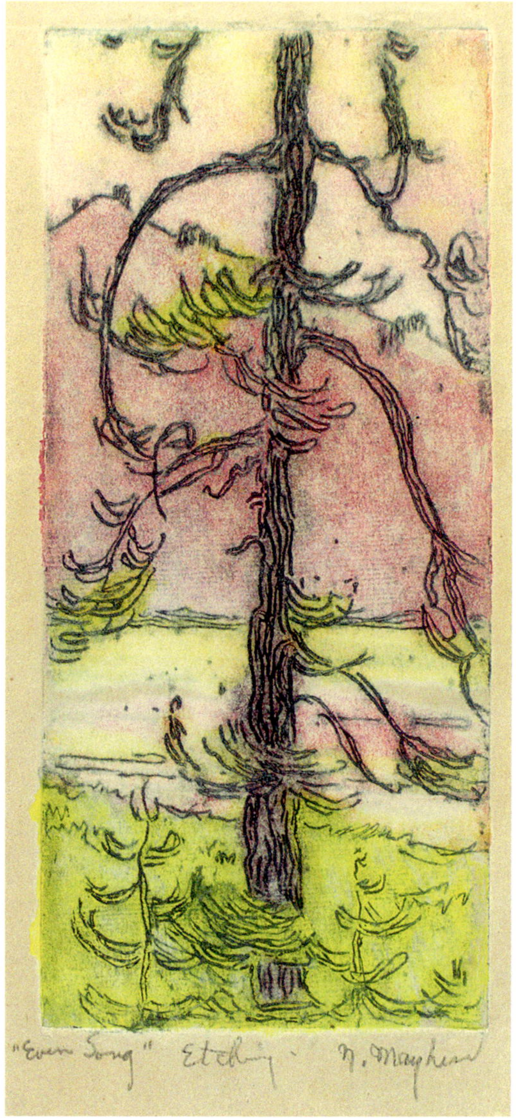

Even Song
c. 1920, Color etching, 8.75" x 3.75"

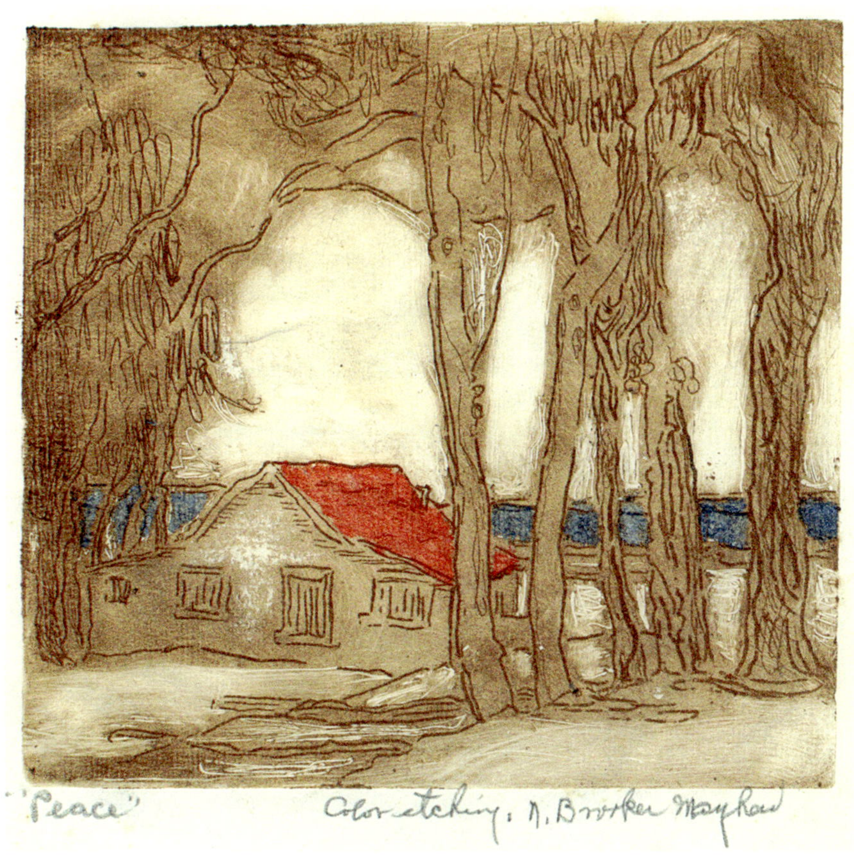

Peace
c. 1915, Color etching, 6.25" x 6.5"
Collection of Mary Furner

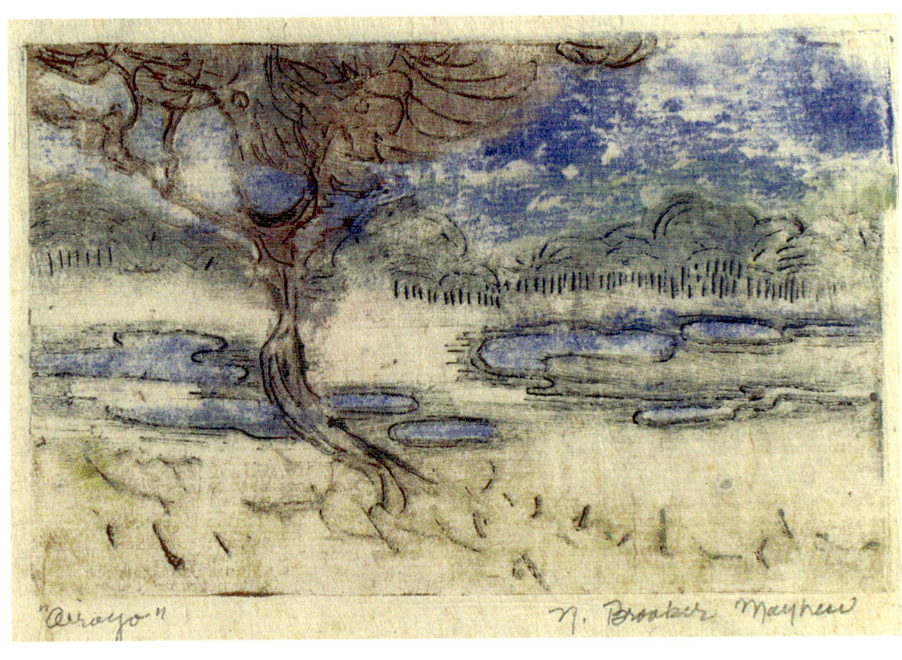

Arroyo
c. 1920s, 4.75" x 7.5"

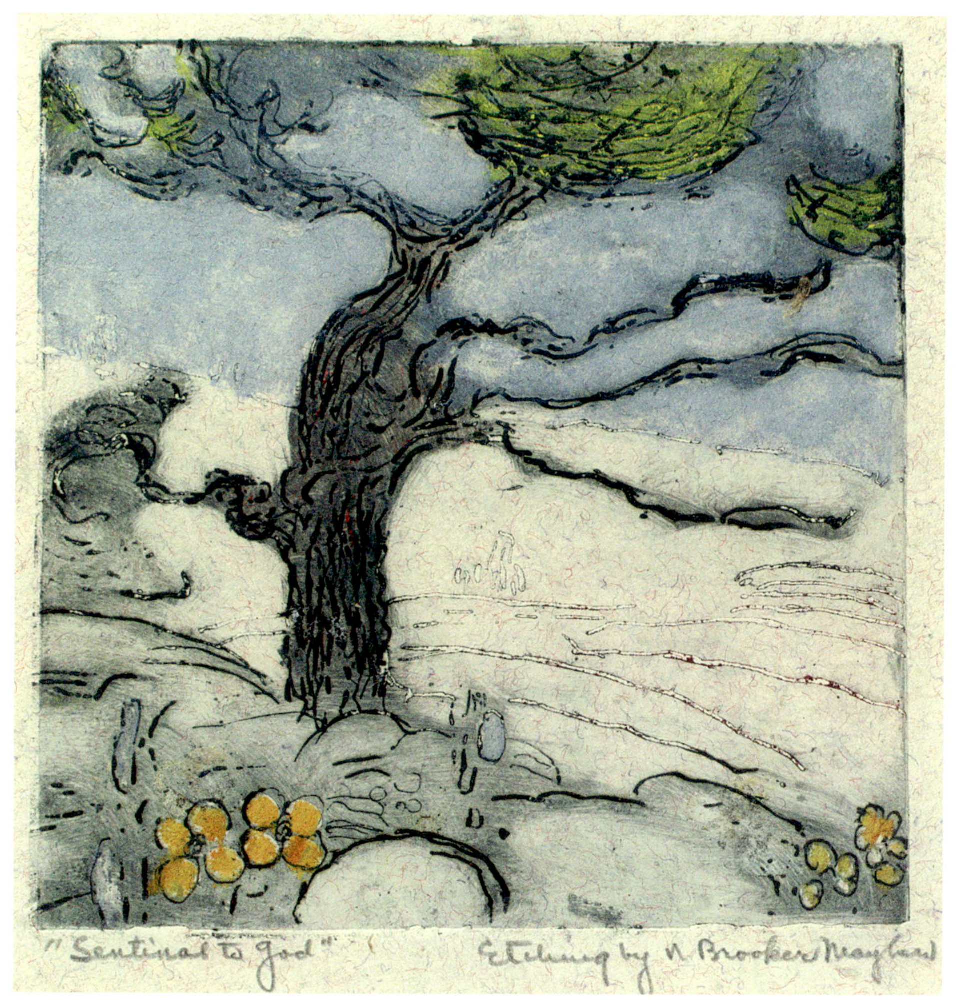

Sentinel to God
c. 1915, 7.25" x 7"

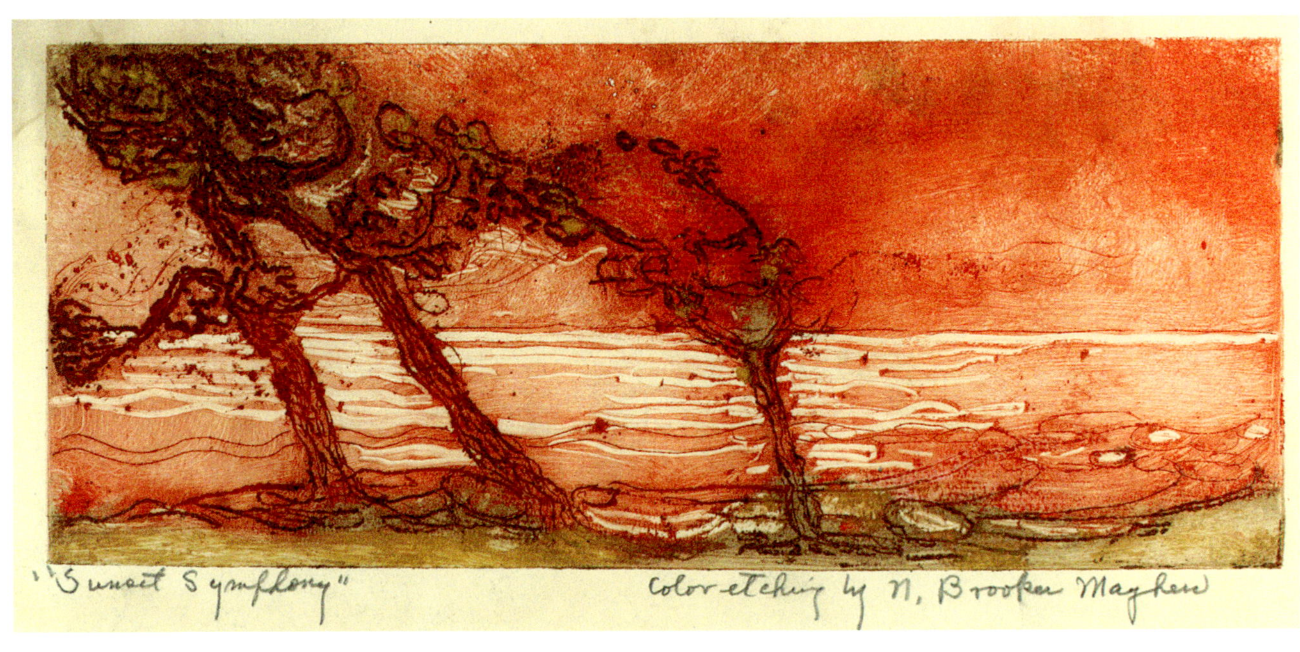

Sunset Symphony
c. 1910, Color etching, 3.25" x 9"

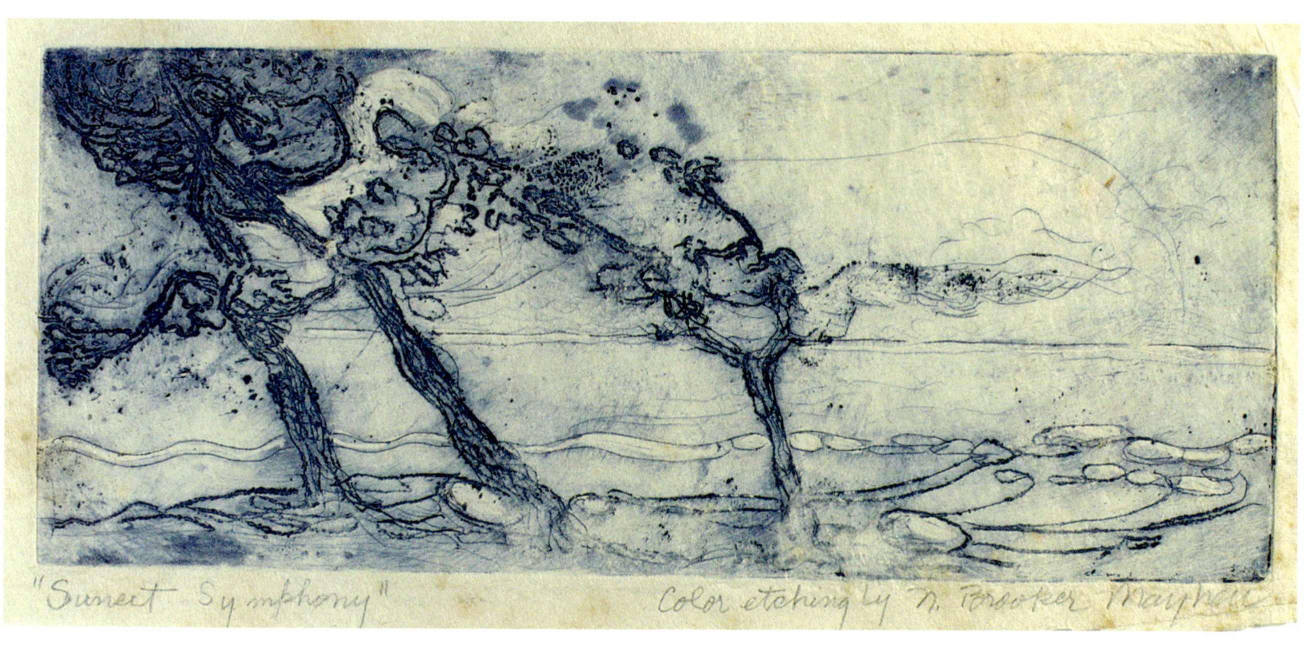

Sunset Symphony
c. 1910, Color etching, 3.25" x 9"

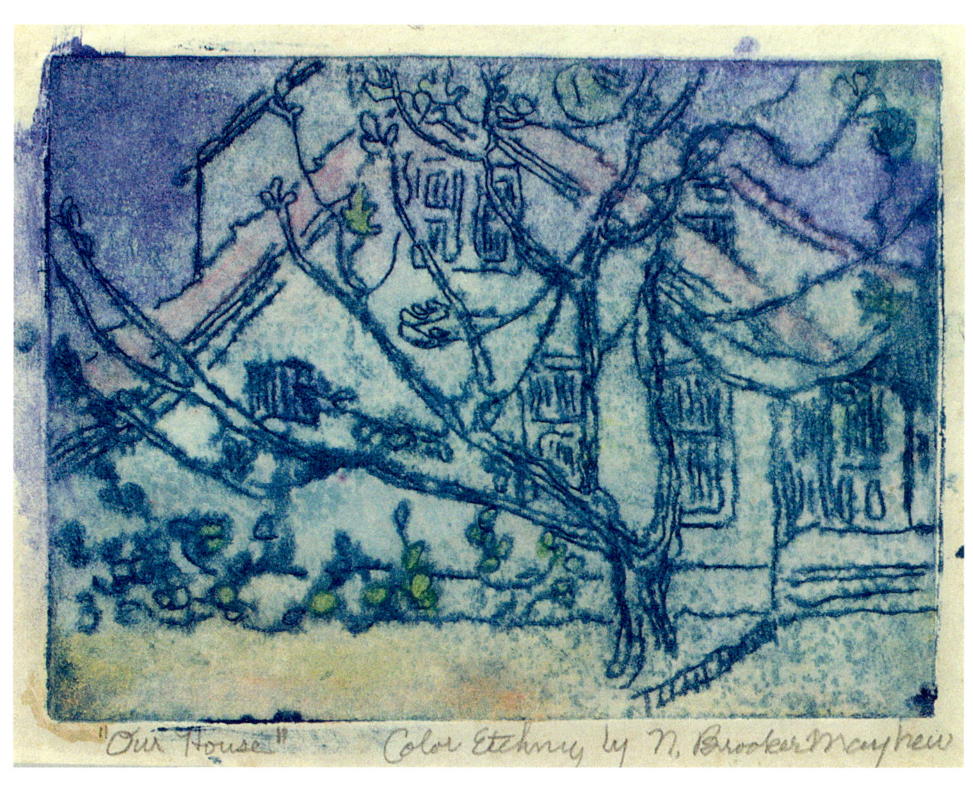

Our House
n.d., Color etching, 5" x 6.5"

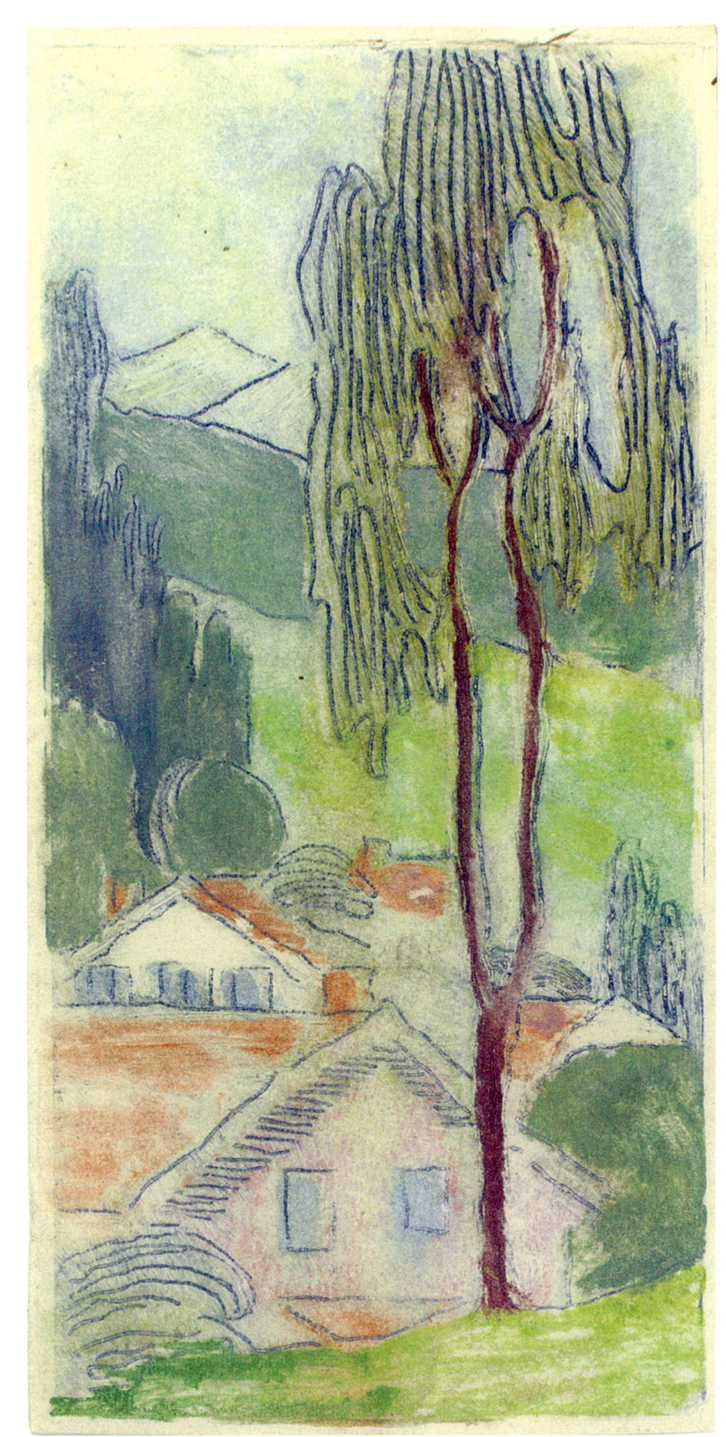

Housetops
c. 1915, Color etching, 9.5" x 4.5"

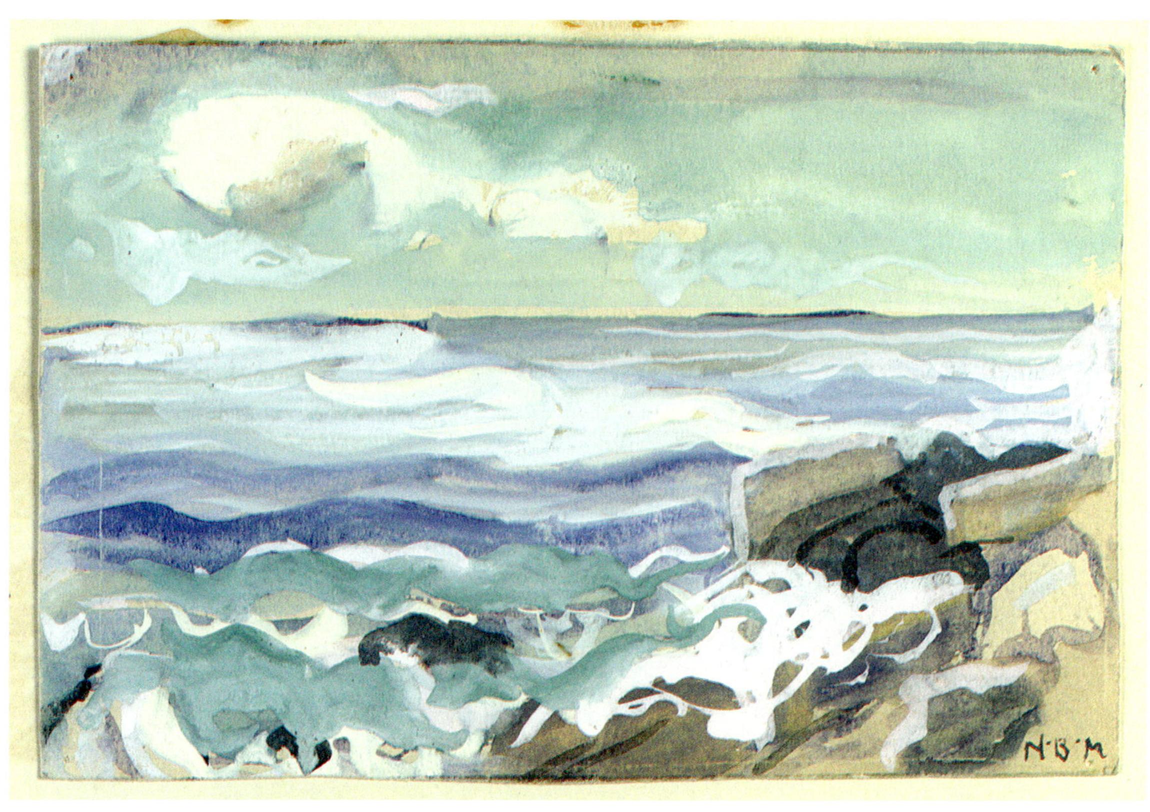

Sunset Symphony
c. 1910, Watercolor on paper, 5" x 7"

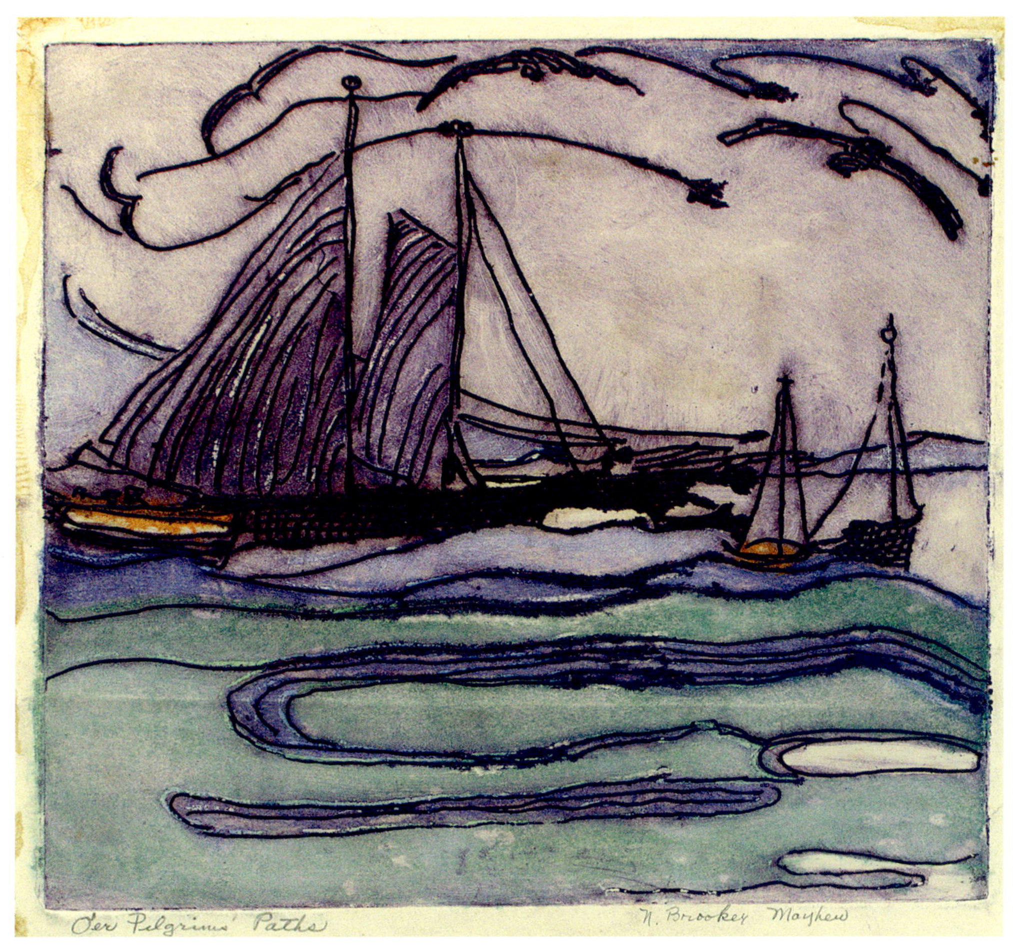

O'er Pilgrim's Paths
c. 1900, Color etching, 7.5" x 8"

Chronology

1875	Born in Astoria, IL April 17
1895–1897	Northwestern University, Illinois, Bachelor of Science
1899	Post-graduate work at Chicago University, IL (University of Chicago)
1901–1906	Post-graduate work at University of Illinois Champaign Urbana, IL
1902	Marriage to Sidney Brooker October 15
1903	Sidney Brooker dies July 4
1905–1906	Attends Chicago Art Institute, IL
1908	Moves to Los Angeles, CA
1910–1915	Instructor at College of Fine Arts, Garvanza (now University of Southern California)
1911	Marriage to Leonard Mayhew
1911	Birth of Mary Jane Mayhew
1914	Birth of Nell Mayhew
1921	Travels for California Mission Series
1926	Divorce from Leonard Mayhew
1930	Automobile trip to East Coast, sketching
1940	Dies in Los Angeles, CA September 24

Collections

Pasadena Public Library
Pasadena, CA

Memorial Library
Ashton, IL*

Sullivan Goss Private Collection
Santa Barbara, CA

Architectural Club of Illinois
Chicago, IL*

California State Library
Sacramento, CA

Gibson, Dunn, and Crutcher, LLP
Los Angeles, CA

First Unitarian Church
Los Angeles, CA*

Highland Park Ebell Club
Highland Park, CA*

Santa Barbara Museum of Art
Santa Barbara, CA

Smithsonian American Art Museum
Washington, D.C.

Ambassador Hotel
Los Angeles, CA*

Mr. Mark Sailor
Santa Barbara, CA

Mr. Roger Genser
Santa Barbara, CA

Mr. and Mrs. Robert Duffy
Los Angeles, CA

Mr. and Mrs. Edward and Nell Kemble
Santa Barbara, CA

Ms. Mary Jane Barton
Santa Barbara, CA

* Pieces missing or lost

Exhibitions

1892
Art Institute of Chicago
Group Exhibition
Chicago, IL

1906
Art Institute of Chicago
Annual Exhibition
Chicago, IL

1907
Art Institute of Chicago
Annual Exhibition
Chicago, IL

1908
Blanchard Gallery
Solo Exhibition
Los Angeles, CA

1909
Alaska-Yukon Exposition
Medal Winner
Seattle, WA

1909
Blanchard Gallery
Solo Exhibition
Los Angeles, CA

1909/1910
Chautauqua Exhibition
Long Beach, CA

1910
College of Fine Arts Garvanza (USC)
Solo Exhibition
Los Angeles, CA

1911
Blanchard Gallery
Solo Exhibition
Los Angeles, CA

1911
College of Fine Arts Garvanza (USC)
Solo Exhibition
Los Angeles, CA

1912
Southwestern Painters
Group Exhibition
Los Angeles, CA

1912
Blanchard Gallery
Solo Exhibition
Los Angeles, CA

1912
Daniell Gallery
Solo Exhibition
Los Angeles, CA

1912
College of Fine Arts Garvanza (USC)
Los Angeles, CA

1913
Anderson Gallery
Solo Exhibition
Chicago, IL

1914
California Art Club
Group Exhibition
Los Angeles, CA

1915
Blanchard Gallery
Group Exhibition
Los Angeles, CA

1915
Chicago Society of Etchers
Art Institute of Chicago
Chicago, IL

1916
Long Beach Memorial Library
Solo Exhibition
Los Angeles, CA

1916
College Woman's Club
Solo Exhibition
Los Angeles, CA

1916
Print Makers of Los Angeles
Group Exhibition
Los Angeles, CA

1916
California State Fair
Sacramento, CA

1917
Arizona State Fair
Phoenix, AZ

1917
Print Makers of Los Angeles
Group Exhibition
Los Angeles, CA

1917
California Art Club
Group Exhibition
Los Angeles, CA

1918
California Art Club
Group Exhibition
Los Angeles, CA

1918
Print Makers of Los Angeles
Group Exhibition
Los Angeles, CA

1919
Chicago Society of Etchers
Art Institute of Chicago
Chicago, IL

1919
Print Makers of Los Angeles
Group Exhibition
Los Angeles, CA

1919
California Art Club
Annual Gold Medal Exposition
Los Angeles, CA

1920
Pasadena Public Library
Solo Exhibition
Los Angeles, CA

1920
Woman's Club of Hollywood
Los Angeles, CA

1920
California Art Club
Annual Gold Medal Exposition
Los Angeles, CA

1921
Hollywood Art Shop Exhibit
Hollywood, CA

1921
The Print Makers of California
Group Exhibition
Los Angeles, CA

1921
Ambassador Hotel
108 Color Etchings displayed
Los Angeles, CA

1921
Ambassador Hotel
94 Color Etchings displayed
New York, NY

1924
Sierra Madre Women's Club
Los Angeles, CA

1924
Women's University Club
Group Exhibition
Los Angeles, CA

1924
Federated Women's Clubs
Los Angeles, CA

1924
Donaldson Studio
Solo Exhibition
Los Angeles, CA

1924
Barker Brothers
Solo Exhibition
Los Angeles, CA

1925
MacDowell Club of Allied Arts
Los Angeles, CA

1926
The Society of Independent Artists
New York, NY

1926
The National Arts Club Exhibition of Living American Etchers
New York, NY

1926
The West Coast Arts Exhibition
Los Angeles, CA

1926
California State Fair
Sacramento, CA

1927
California State Fair
Sacramento, CA

1927
Solo Exhibition at Mayhew home
Los Angeles, CA

1927
The West Coast Arts Exhibition
Los Angeles, CA

1928
Laguna Beach Art Association
Group Exhibition
Laguna Beach, CA

1928
Pacific Southwest Exposition
Group Exhibition
Long Beach, CA

1928
California State Fair
Sacramento, CA

1928
Santa Cruz Art League
Santa Cruz, CA
1928
Gardena High School
Group Exhibition
Gardena, CA

1929
California State Exhibition
Sacramento, CA

1929
Laguna Beach Art Gallery
Group Exhibition
Laguna Beach, CA

1930
Gardena High School
Group Exhibition
Gardena, CA

1930
Purchase Prize Exhibition of Paintings
Palos Verdes, CA

1931
Barker Brothers Artists
Fiesta Exhibition
Los Angeles, CA

1931
Gardena High School
Group Exhibition
Gardena, CA

1931
Pasadena Art Institute
Group Exhibition
Pasadena, CA

1931
Purchase Prize Exhibition of Paintings
Palos Verdes, CA

1932
Gardena High School
Group Exhibition
Gardena, CA

1932
Ebell Salon of Art
Group Exhibition
Los Angeles, CA

1933
Gardena High School
Group Exhibition
Gardena, CA

1934
Gardena High School
Group Exhibition
Gardena, CA

1934
Laguna Beach Art Association
Group Exhibition
Laguna Beach, CA

1934
Women Painters of the West
Group Exhibition
Los Angeles, CA

1935
National Housing Exhibition
Group Exhibition

1935
National Gallery of Art
Smithsonian American Art Museum Exhibition
Washington, D.C.

All Known Exhibited Works

The Adobe
1928
California State Fair
Sacramento, CA
The California State
Library Collection

Afternoon
1909/1910
Chautauqua Exhibition
Long Beach, CA

Afternoon Fog
1911
College of Fine Arts Garvanza (USC)
Solo Exhibition
Los Angeles, CA

After the Rain
1911
College of Fine Arts Garvanza (USC)
Solo Exhibition
Los Angeles, CA

April Morn
1915
Chicago Society of Etchers
Art Institute of Chicago
Chicago, IL

1917
Print Makers of Los Angeles
Group Exhibition
Los Angeles, CA

April Sycamores
1912
College of Fine Arts Garvanza (USC)
Los Angeles, CA

The Arroyo in Spring /
Spring in the Arroyo
1911
College of Fine Arts Garvanza (USC)
Solo Exhibition
Los Angeles, CA

1912
Southwestern Painters
Group Exhibition
Los Angeles, CA

Arroyo Seco
1935
National Gallery of Art
(Smithsonian American Art Museum)

Arroyo Sycamores
1911
College of Fine Arts Garvanza (USC)
Solo Exhibition
Los Angeles, CA

At Laguna
1925
MacDowell Club of Allied Arts
Los Angeles, CA

At San Pedro
1909/1910
Chautauqua Exhibition
Long Beach, CA

Autumn Gold
1906
Art Institute of Chicago
Annual Exhibition
Chicago, IL

Autumn Lyric
1925
MacDowell Club of Allied Arts
Los Angeles, CA

A Bit of Arcadia
1919
Print Makers of Los Angeles
Group Exhibition
Los Angeles, CA

Blue and Gold
1919
California Art Club
Los Angeles, CA

By the Sea
1909/1910
Chautauqua Exhibition
Long Beach, CA

1917
Arizona State Fair
Phoenix, AZ

1918
Laguna Beach Art Gallery Group
Exhibition
Laguna Beach, CA

1918
Print Makers of Los Angeles
Group Exhibition
Los Angeles, CA

California Gold
1928
Santa Cruz Art League
Santa Cruz, CA

1931
Barker Brother
Artists Fiesta Exhibition
Los Angeles, CA

California March
1925
MacDowell Club of Allied Arts
Los Angeles, CA

California Mission, San Jose
1926
The National Arts Club
Exhibition of Living American Etchers
New York, NY

A California Poppy Field
1912
College of Fine Arts Garvanza (USC)
Los Angeles, CA

California Water
1931
Barker Brothers
Artists Fiesta Exhibition
Los Angeles, CA

Capistrano
1921
The Print Makers of California
Group Exhibition
Los Angeles, CA

Catalina
1909/1910
Chautauqua Exhibition
Long Beach, CA
Cloudy Valley
1921
Hollywood Art Shop
Exhibit Hollywood, CA

The Coming Fog
1911
College of Fine Arts Garvanza (USC)
Solo Exhibition
Los Angeles, CA

Courage
1924
Barker Brothers
Solo Exhibition
Los Angeles, CA

The Dusty Road
1915
Blanchard Gallery
Group Exhibition
Los Angeles, CA

Eucalyptus
1909/1910
Chautauqua Exhibition
Long Beach, CA

Evening Comes
1916
Print Makers of Los Angeles
Group Exhibition
Los Angeles, CA

1916
California State Fair
Sacramento, CA

1924
Barker Brothers
Solo Exhibition
Los Angeles, CA

Evening Eucalyptus
1916
Print Makers of Los Angeles
Group Exhibition
Los Angeles, CA

1916
California State Fair
Sacramento, CA

Flower Decoration
1935
National Housing Exhibition
Group Exhibition

Flower Panel
1931
Barker Brothers
Artists Fiesta Exhibition
Los Angeles, CA

Foot-hill Lyric
1919
California Art Club
Los Angeles, CA

From my Garden
1928
Pacific Southwest Exposition
Group Exhibition
Long Beach, CA

Garvanza House Tops
1917
Print Makers of Los Angeles
Group Exhibition
Los Angeles, CA

1917
Arizona State Fair
Phoenix, AZ

A Gillesque Fragment
1919
Print Makers of Los Angeles
Group Exhibition
Los Angeles, CA

The Gloaming
1917
Print Makers of Los Angeles
Group Exhibition
Los Angeles, CA

The Golden Hush
1912
College of Fine Arts Garvanza (USC)
Los Angeles, CA

Happy Valley
1919
California Art Club
Los Angeles, CA

The Harbor
1909/1910
Chautauqua Exhibition
Long Beach, CA

Homeward Bound
1917
Print Makers of Los Angeles
Group Exhibition
Los Angeles, CA

1924
Barker Brothers
Solo Exhibition
Los Angeles, CA

In Silhouette
1912
College of Fine Arts Garvanza (USC)
Los Angeles, CA

In the Yellow Hush, Back East

1918
Laguna Beach Art Gallery
Group Exhibition
Laguna Beach, CA

1918
Print Makers
of Los Angeles
Group Exhibition
Los Angeles, CA

Jeweled Cove
1929
Laguna Beach Art Gallery
Group Exhibition
Laguna Beach, CA

Jeweled Spring
1925
MacDowell Club of Allied Arts
Los Angeles, CA

1926
California State Fair
Sacramento, CA

1928
Gardena High School
Group Exhibition
Gardena, CA

Lone Tree
1921
The Print Makers of California
Group Exhibition
Los Angeles, CA

Mate of the Mountain Wind
1925
MacDowell Club of Allied Arts
Los Angeles, CA

Mission Dolores
1926
The National Arts Club
Exhibition of Living American Etchers
New York, NY

Mission Dolores, San Francisco
Isenberg & Associates, Inc.
Collection

Mission San Buenaventura
Isenberg & Associates, Inc.
Collection

Mission San Carlos
Isenberg & Associates, Inc.
Collection

Mission San Luis Obispo
Isenberg & Associates, Inc.
Collection

Mission San Luis Rey
Isenberg & Associates, Inc.
Collection

Mission San Juan Batista
1924
Barker Brothers
Solo Exhibition
Los Angeles, CA

Mission Santa Barbara
Isenberg & Associates, Inc.
Collection

Mission Sonoma
Isenberg & Associates, Inc.
Collection

Monrovia Meadows
1911
College of Fine Arts Garvanza (USC)
Solo Exhibition
Los Angeles, CA

Morning on the Kalamazoo River
1909
Alaska-Yukon Exposition
Medal Winner
Seattle, WA

Morning on the River, Back East
1918
Laguna Beach Art Gallery
Group Exhibition
Laguna Beach, CA

1918
Print Makers of Los Angeles
Group Exhibition
Los Angeles, CA

Mooring the Boats
1915
Blanchard Gallery
Group Exhibition
Los Angeles, CA

Mt. Washington in Mist
1933
Gardena High School
Group Exhibition
Gardena, CA

Oak Hill
1909/1910
Chautauqua Exhibition
Long Beach, CA

Ode to Spring
1928
California State Fair
Sacramento, CA

Panel for a Mural
1918
California Art Club
Group Exhibition
Los Angeles, CA

The Patriotic Garden
1917
Arizona State Fair
Phoenix, AZ

A Peaceful Path
1912
Southwestern Painters
Group Exhibition
Los Angeles, CA

The Philosopher
1917
California Art Club
Group Exhibition
Los Angeles, CA

Rest
1916
Print Makers of Los Angeles
Group Exhibition
Los Angeles, CA

1916
California State Fair
Sacramento, CA

San Diego Mission, California
1926
The Society of Independent Artists
New York, NY

Isenberg & Associates, Inc.
Collection

San Gabriel Mission
1909
Blanchard Gallery
Solo Exhibition
Los Angeles, CA

Sand and Snow
1934
Women Painters of the West
Group Exhibition
Los Angeles, CA

Sand Dunes
1909
Alaska-Yukon Exposition
Medal Winner
Seattle, WA

1915
Chicago Society of Etchers
Art Institute of Chicago
Chicago, IL

1917
Print Makers of Los Angeles
Group Exhibition
Los Angeles, CA

Santa Inez Mission, California
1926
The Society of Independent Artists
New York, NY

Isenberg & Associates, Inc.
Collection

The Ship
1912
College of Fine Arts Garvanza (USC)
Los Angeles, CA

Sierra's Golden Garden
1912
College of Fine Arts Garvanza (USC)
Los Angeles, CA

The Silver Sea
1912
College of Fine Arts Garvanza (USC)
Los Angeles, CA

1921
Hollywood Art Shop Exhibit
Hollywood, CA

1932
Ebell Salon of Art
Group Exhibition
Los Angeles, CA

The Smiling Pool
1925
MacDowell Club of Allied Arts
Los Angeles, CA

Snow and Flowers
1934
Laguna Beach Art Association
Group Exhibition
Laguna Beach, CA

Song of the Waves
1931
Gardena High School
Group Exhibition
Gardena, CA

Spanish Isle
Santa Barbara Museum of Art
Santa Barbara, CA

Spring
1931
Palos Verde's Public Library and
Art Gallery
Group Exhibition
Palos Verdes, CA

1932
The Fifth Purchase
Prize Exhibition
Gardena High School
Gardena, CA

A Street in San Gabriel
1912
Southwestern Painters
Group Exhibition
Los Angeles, CA

A Summer Day, Back East
1918
Laguna Beach Art Gallery
Group Exhibition
Laguna Beach, CA

1918
Print Makers of Los Angeles
Group Exhibition
Los Angeles, CA

Summer's Day in Illinois
1912
College of Fine Arts Garvanza (USC)
Los Angeles, CA

Sunrise at the Edge of the Desert
1931
Pasadena Art Institute
Group Exhibition
Pasadena, CA

Sunset
1907
Art Institute of Chicago
Annual Exhibition
Chicago, IL

Sunshine
1912
College of Fine Arts Garvanza (USC)
Los Angeles, CA

The Tale of Time
1914
California Art Club
Group Exhibition
Los Angeles, CA

The Tapestry of Spring
1934
Gardena High School
Group Exhibition
Gardena, CA

The Temple of the Gods
1927
California State Fair
Sacramento, CA

To a Silver Morning
1926
The West Coast Arts
Exhibition
Los Angeles, CA

1927
The West Coast Arts
Exhibition
Los Angeles, CA

1930
Purchase Prize
Exhibition of Paintings
Palos Verdes, CA

Torrey Pines
1925
MacDowell Club of Allied Arts
Los Angeles, CA

1926
California State Fair
Sacramento, CA

Tree and Hillside
Santa Barbara Museum of Art
Santa Barbara, CA

Twin Oaks
1909/1910
Chautauqua Exhibition
Long Beach, CA

Valley Sentinels
1911
College of Fine Art Garvanza (USC)
Solo Exhibition
Los Angeles, CA

1911
Blanchard Gallery
Solo Exhibition
Los Angeles, CA

1912
College of Fine Arts Garvanza (USC)
Los Angeles, CA

The Vicarage
1909/1910
Chautauqua Exhibition
Long Beach, CA

The Village Street
1920
Annual Gold Medal Exposition
Los Angeles, CA

The Workman's Cottage
1919
Chicago Society of Etchers
Art Institute of Chicago
Chicago, IL

1919
Print Makers of Los Angeles
Group Exhibition
Los Angeles, CA

1928
Laguna Beach Art Association
Group Exhibition
Laguna Beach, CA

Yacht
1892
Art Institute of Chicago's
Annual Exhibition of Watercolors
by American Artists

Bibliography

Acton, David
A Spectrum of Innovation: Color in American Printmaking 1890–1960
Worcester, MA
Worcester Art Museum
1990

Alaska Yukon-Pacific Exhibition
Fine Arts Gallery and Exhibit of Arts and Crafts
Seattle, WA
1909

Barton, Mary Jane and Nell Kemble
Interview by Alissa Anderson
Santa Barbara, CA
April 2003

Anderson, Anthony
"Art and Artists"
Los Angeles Times
21 May 1911

Anderson, Anthony
"Art and Artists"
Los Angeles Times
2 June 1912

Anderson, Anthony
"Art and Artists"
Los Angeles Times
20 October 1912

Anderson, Anthony
"Art and Artists"
Los Angeles Times
17 November 1912

Anderson, Anthony
"Art and Artists"
Los Angeles Times
25 April 1915

Anderson, Anthony
"Art and Artists"
Los Angeles Times
27 August 1916

Anderson, Anthony
"Art and Artists"
Los Angeles Times
17 September 1916

Anderson, Anthony
"Art and Artists"
Los Angeles Times
17 December 1916

Anderson, Anthony
"Art and Artists"
Los Angeles Times
22 February 1920

Anderson, Anthony
"Art and Artists"
Los Angeles Times
23 January 1921

Anderson, Anthony
"Art and Artists"
Los Angeles Times
3 February 1924

Anderson, Anthony
"Of Art and Artists"
Los Angeles Times
2 March 1924

Annual Exhibition Record of the Art Institute of Chicago
Champaign-Urbana, IL
Champaign Public Library
n.d.

"Art and Artists"
(Los Angeles) Graphic
11 December 1909

Art Institute of Chicago
"Catalogue of Students 1904–1905"
Chicago, IL
1905

Art Inventory for "Nell Brooker Mayhew"
Smithsonian Institution Research Information System
February 2003

"Art Renting Plan Approved"
Los Angeles Examiner
18 January 1931

Artists Listing
Record for Highland Park District, Los Angeles. Arroyo Seco Branch, Los Angeles Public Library

"The Ashton Story"
Local History File, Mills-Petrie Memorial Library
Ashton, IL

"Calendar Listing"
California Southland
July 1924

"Calendar Listing"
California Southland
August 1924

"Calendar Listing"
California Southland
November 1924

"Calendar Listing"
California Southland
December 1924

"Calendar Listing"
California Southland
March 1925

"Calendar Listing"
California Southland
June 1925

"Calendar Listing"
California Southland
December 1925

"Calendar Listing"
California Southland
November 1927

"Calendar Listing"
California Southland
January 1929

The California Art Club
8th Annual Exhibition
Los Angeles, CA
October 1917
Ferdinant Perret Papers, Archives of American Art, Smithsonian Institution, Roll # 3866, Frame 1017

The California Art Club
Spring Exhibition
Los Angeles, CA
April 1918
Ferdinant Perret Papers, Archives of American Art, Smithsonian Institution, Roll # 3866, Frame 1072

The California Art Club
Exhibition
Los Angeles, CA
1914
Ferdinant Perret Papers, Archives of American Art, Smithsonian Institution, Roll # 3866, Frame 786

"California Arts and Architecture"
Artist's Fiesta
Santa Barbara, CA
September 1931

California State Fair
"Annual Exhibition of Paintings"
Sacramento, CA
September 1926
Ferdinant Perret Papers, Archives of American Art, Smithsonian Institution, Roll # 3867, Frame 775

California State Fair
"Annual Exhibition of Paintings"
Sacramento, CA
September 1927
Ferdinant Perret Papers, Archives of American Art, Smithsonian Institution, Roll # 3866, Frame 1015

California State Fair
"Annual Exhibition of Paintings"
Sacramento, CA
September 1927
Ferdinant Perret Papers, Archives of American Art, Smithsonian Institution, Roll # 3867, Frame 1015

California State Fair
"Annual Exhibition of Paintings"
Sacramento, CA
September 1928
Ferdinant Perret Papers, Archives of American Art, Smithsonian Institution, Roll # 3866, Frame 1291

"Catalogue of Invited Works by Painters, Sculptors, and Craftsmen"
Pacific Southwest Exhibition Catalogue
Long Beach, CA
July / September 1928
Ferdinant Perret Papers, Archives of American Art, Smithsonian Institution, Roll # 3867, Frame 1253

"The College of Fine Arts Faculty Listing"
University of Southern California Bulletin: Year Book for 1912–1913
March 1913
Vol. VIII No. 1

Collins, Jim and Glenn B. Opitz, eds.
Women Artists in America
Poughkeepsie, NY
Apollo
1980

Culley, John H
"Woodblock Prints and Their Makers"
The Argus: A Journal of Art
July / August 1928

Danely, Nellie
Alumni Record
Northwestern University Library Archives
1895–1941

"Decorative Studies at MacDowell Club"
Los Angeles Times
29 November 1925

"Definition of Aesthetic movement"
29 June 2003
http://www.webdesk.com/quotations/aes.html

De Quelin, Rene T.
"Art and Artists"
(Los Angeles) Graphic
7 November 1908

"Directory of California Artists, Craftsmen, Designers, and Etchers."
California Arts and Architecture
December 1932

Ebell Salon of Art
"Third Annual Exhibition of California Painters and Sculptors"
Los Angeles, CA
Ebell
1932
Ferdinant Perret Papers, Archives of American Art, Smithsonian Institution, Roll # 3869, Frame 754

"Exhibition of Paintings"
The West Coast Arts Exhibition Catalogue
Los Angeles, CA
29 January 1927
Ferdinant Perret Papers, Archives of American Art, Smithsonian Institution, Roll # 3867, Frame 882

Falk, Peter Hastings, ed.
Annual Exhibition Record of th Art Institute of Chicago 1888–1950
Madison, CT
Sound View Press
1990

Falk, Peter, et al.
Who Was Who in American Art
Madison, CT
Sound View Press
1999

The Five Friendly Valleys: The Story of Greater Highland Park
Los Angeles, CA
Highland Park Branch Security Trust and Savings Bank
1923

"Funeral of Art Teacher Scheduled"
Los Angeles Times
26 September 1940

Gardena High School
"Purchase Prize Exhibit Catalogue of Paintings"
Gardena, CA
April 1928
Ferdinant Perret Papers, Archives of American Art, Smithsonian Institution, Roll # 3867, Frame 1174

Gardena High School
"Purchase Prize Exhibit Catalogue of Paintings"
Gardena, CA
April / May 1930
Ferdinant Perret Papers, Archives of American Art, Smithsonian Institution, Roll # 3868, Frame 504

Gardena High School
"Purchase Prize Exhibit Catalogue of Paintings"
Gardena, CA
April 1931
Ferdinant Perret Papers, Archives of American Art, Smithsonian Institution, Roll # 3868, Frame 1041

Gardena High School
"Purchase Prize Exhibit Catalogue of Paintings"
Gardena, CA
March / April 1932
Ferdinant Perret Papers, Archives of American Art, Smithsonian Institution, Roll # 3869, Frame 626

Gardena High School
"The Seventh Purchase Prize Exhibit"
Gardena, CA
April 1934
Ferdinant Perret Papers, Archives of American Art, Smithsonian Institution, Roll # 3870, Frame 901

Gardena High School
"The Sixth Purchase Prize Exhibit"
Gardena, CA
April / May 1933
Ferdinant Perret Papers, Archives of American Art, Smithsonian Institution, Roll # 3870, Frame 168

Goss, Tyler Sullivan
Nell Brooker Mayhew: Master of the Color Etching and California Painter
Santa Barbara, CA
Sullivan Goss, Ltd.
circa 2002

Green, Nancy E
"Arthur Wesley Dow: American Arts and Crafts"
American Art Review
November / December 1999

Green, Nancy E. and Jessie Poesch
Arthur Wesley Dow and American Arts and Crafts
New York
The American Federation of Arts
1999

Hill, Alden Lee
"William Lees Judson"
The Highlands of Los Angeles
Radio Show
20 March 193
University of Southern California Archives

Hughes, Edan Milton
Artists in California: 1786–1940, vol. II
San Francisco
Hughes Publishing Company
1989

Isenberg, Michelle
E-mail to GRM listing eleven prints owned by Gibson, Dunn, and Crutcher
2003

"John Johansen biography"
AskArt.com
n.d.
http://www.askart.com/biography.asp

"John Vanderpoel biography"
AskArt.com
n.d.
http://www.askart.com/biography.asp

Kaplan, Wendy
The Art That is Life
Boston, MA
Museum of Fine Arts
1987

Kovinick, Phil and Marian Yoshiki-Kovinick
An Encyclopedia of Women Artists of the American West
Austin, TX
University of Texas Press
1998

Laguna Beach Art Association
Exhibition Catalogue
August / September 1934

Laguna Beach Art Association
10th Anniversary Souvenir: 1918–1928
Laguna Beach, CA
27 July 1928
Ferdinant Perret Papers, Archives of American Art, Smithsonian Institution, Roll # 3866, Frame 1115

Laguna Beach Art Gallery
Exhibition Catalogue
Laguna Beach
16 February 1929
Ferdinant Perret Papers, Archives of American Art, Smithsonian Institution, Roll # 3868, Frame 10

"Laguna Beach Colony Notes"
Laguna Beach Life
24 July 1924
8 col. 2.
(GRM would like to thank Joan Moreno, Laguna Beach Branch Library and Nancy Dustin Wall Moure for bringing this citation to her attention.)

Langdale, Cecily
Monotypes by Maurice Prendergast in the Terra Museum of American Art
Chicago, IL
The Terra Museum of American Art
1984

"Library Home Now Almost Complete"
Pasadena Star-News
2 November 1922

"List of Instructors for the College of Fine Art."
University of Southern California Bulletin and Yearbook
Los Angeles, CA
1912–1913

Los Angeles Art Association
List of Committee members
1934
Ferdinant Perret Papers, Archives of American Art, Smithsonian Institution, Roll # 3870, Frame 1062

Mallett, Daniel Trowbridge
Mallett's Index of Artists
New York, NY
Peter Smith
1948

Marlor, Clark S
The Society of Independent Artists: The Exhibition Record 1917–1944
Park Ridge, NJ
Noyes Press
1984

Maxwell, Everett C
"Art"
(Los Angeles) Graphic
22 October 1910

Maxwell, Everett C
"Art"
(Los Angeles) Graphic
8 April 1911

Maxwell, Everett C
"Art"
(Los Angeles) Graphic
27 May 1911

Mayhew, N.B.
"Nell Brooker Mayhew; Painter, Etcher."
Marketing Flyer
Found at Los Angeles Public Library
n.d.

"Mayhew, Nell B."
California State Library
Occupational Index Cards
1918

Mayhew, Nell Brooker
Announcing a Series of Art Lectures and an Exhibition of Color Etchings
Marketing Flyer
n.d.

Mayhew, Nell Brooker
"Preserving Wild Flowers"
Los Angeles Times
14 April 1916

Mayhew, Nell Brooker
"Prints for the Small House"
California Southland
February 1925

"Mayhew Pictures to be seen at Library"
Pasadena Star-News
6 February 1920

Meech, Julia and Gabriel P. Weisberg
Japonisme Comes to America: The Japanese Impact on the Graphic Arts 1876–1925
New York, NY
Harry N. Abrams, Inc.
1990

"Memorial Building Combines Artistic Harmony, Efficiency"
Ashton (Illinois) Gazette
2 July 1936

Merrell, Eric
"California Art Club"
E-mail of exhibitions to GRM
2003

The Metropolitan Museum of Art
The Painterly Print
New York, NY
The Metropolitan Museum of Art
1981

Millier, Arthur
"Color is Feature of Mayhew Prints"
Los Angeles Times
13 July 1924

"National Housing Exposition"
18 May 1935
Ferdinant Perret Papers, Archives of American Art, Smithsonian Institution, Roll # 3872, Frame 9

"Nell Brooker Mayhew"
The Western Woman
March 1939
Vol. IX No. 8
Ferdinant Perret Papers, Archives of American Art, Smithsonian Institution, Roll # 3860, Frame 790

Northwestern University Record of Alumni Accomplishments
Northwestern University Archives
Questionnaire and Clipping File

"Of Art and Artists"
Los Angeles Times
27 December 1925

Opitz, Glenn, ed.
Mantle Fielding's Dictionary of American Painters. 2nd ed.
Poughkeepsie, NY
Apollo
1986

Palos Verdes Public Library and Art Gallery
Second Annual Purchase Prize Exhibition of Paintings
Palos Verdes, CA
February / April 1931
Ferdinant Perret Papers, Archives of American Art, Smithsonian Institution, Roll # 3867, Frame 1128

Partridge, Roi
"The Art and Craft of Etching"
The Argus: A Journal of Art
July / August 1928

Pasadena Art Institute
Fourth Annual Exhibition by California Artists
Pasadena, CA
January 1931
Ferdinant Perret Papers, Archives of American Art, Smithsonian Institution, Roll # 3868, Frame 896

Patterson, Joby
Bertha E. Jaques and the Chicago Society of Etchers
London
Associated University Presses
2002

Print Makers of Los Angeles
Department of Fine and Applied Arts
March 1919
Archives of American Art, Smithsonian Institution, N538, Frame 431

Print Makers of Los Angeles
Gallery of Fine and Applied Arts
Second Annual Spring Exhibit
June / July 1916
Archives of American Art, Smithsonian Institution, N538, Frame 426

Print Makers of Los Angeles
Third Annual Spring Exhibit
March 1917
Archives of American Art, Smithsonian Institution, N538, Frame 429

Print Makers Society of California
4th Annual Spring Exhibit
March 1918
Ferdinant Perret Papers, Archives of American Art, Smithsonian Institution, Roll # 3866, Frame 1040

Print Makers Society of California
The Second International Print Makers Exhibition
March 1921
Archives of American Art, Smithsonian Institution, Br 18, Frame 243

Santa Cruz Art League
"First Annual State-wide Art Exhibit of Paintings"
Santa Cruz, CA
February 1928
Ferdinant Perret Papers, Archives of American Art, Smithsonian Institution, Roll # 3867, Frame 1112

"The Second Echo of the Olympics"
Women Painters of the West Exhibition Catalogue
July / September 1934
Ferdinant Perret Papers, Archives of American Art, Smithsonian Institution, Roll # 3870, Frame 1329

Southwestern Painters 13th Annual
Exhibition Catalogue
Los Angeles, CA
May 1912
Ferdinant Perret Papers, Archives of American Art, Smithsonian Institution, Roll # 3866, Frame 688

Thomas, Steven
"Glowing Spots of Color: The Growth of the Arts and Crafts Woodblock Print in America"
Style 1900: The Quarterly Journal of the Arts & Crafts Movement
New Jersey, NJ
Summer / Fall 1999

Thudichum, Roberta Balfour
"Nell Brooker Mayhew"
Western Arts
Monterey, CA
February 1926

"Travel and Tourist Supplement"
Long Beach Daily Telegram
November 1917
36, col. 2.
(GRM would like to thank Stephanie Spika-Fox, Long beach Public Library for bringing this to her attention.)

Turner, Steve and Victoria Dailey
Nell Brooker Mayhew: Color Etchings and Paintings
Los Angeles, CA
Turner Dailey Gallery
1989

Western Art Quarterly supplement of exhibition calendar
Los Angeles, CA
April 7 1916
Ferdinant Perret Papers, Archives of American Art, Smithsonian Institution, Roll # 3866, Frame 941

"West Coast Arts Incorporated"
California Southland
October 1924

Wilson, Raymond L.
Index of American Print Exhibitions, 1882–1940
Metuchen, NJ
The Scarecrow Press, Inc.
1988

Women Painters of the West
Membership list
1934–1935
Ferdinant Perret Papers, Archives of American Art, Smithsonian Institution, Roll # 3871, Frame 541

"Woman's Club Program"
Holly Leaves
10 January 1920
(GRM would like to thank Nancy Dustin Wall Moure for bringing this article to her attention.)

Acknowledgments

First and foremost, the author would like to thank Frank Goss. With an exceptional type of kindness, trust and confidence, Mr. Goss gave me the honor of writing this book. His enthusiasm and dedication to the arts have inspired me. It was his commitment to the work of Nell Brooker Mayhew that allowed this book to be written.

I would also like to thank Gloria Rexford Martin — a phenomenal art historian of accuracy and precision. Her research built the historical framework of this book.

I offer additional thanks to: Nell Kemble; Mary Jane Barton; Susan Cary (Archives of American Art); The Art Institute of Chicago Ryerson Burnham Libraries/ Archives; Champaign, Illinois Public Library; Nancy Dustin Wall Moure and CaliforniaArt.com; Victoria Daley (Art Historian); Steve Turner (Art Historian); Matt Kettman (Editor); Laurie Shea (Editor); my family; and everyone at Sullivan Goss and Balcony Press for their professional support and friendship.

Gloria Rexford Martin would like to thank the many people who generously gave of their time and ideas and material:

Kathleen Adrian, Smithsonian American Art Museum; Kay Balue (President), Ebell Club of Los Angeles; Janet Blake (Registrar), Laguna Art Museum;Peter Blank (Librarian), The Art Institute of Chicago; Heather Brodhead (Librarian), Santa Barbara Museum of Art; Claudine Burnett (Librarian), Long Beach Public Library; Mrs. Francis Choate (President) Highland Park Ebell Club; Professor Orville Clarke; Alison Dincola (Library Assistant, Literary Manuscripts), Huntington Library; Jacqueline Dugas (Registrar), Huntington Art Collections; Professor Emeritus Beatrice Farwell; Lita Garcia (Manuscripts Department), Huntington Library; John Gonzales (Senior Librarian, California History Section),California State Library; Marian Heslenfeld (Branch Manager, Malaga Cove Library), Palos Verdes Library District; Susan Hikida (Assistant Archivist), University of Southern California; Barbara Hinde (Collection Manager, Department of Prints and Drawings), The Art Institute of Chicago; Joan Hugh (Librarian), Long Beach Public Library; Michelle Isenberg, Isenberg & Associates; Gasper Jenelle, Oregon State Capitol; Phil Kovinick (Art Historian); Pat Lynagh (Reference Librarian), Smithsonian American Art Museum; Marie McCannon (Library Director), Mills & Petrie Memo5 Building Ashton, IL; Denise Mendez (Librarian), Pasadena Public Library; Eric Merrell (Archivist), California Art Club; Joan Moreno (Librarian), Laguna Beach Branch Library; Joan Moser (Curator of Graphic Arts,) Smithsonian American Art Museum; Nancy Dustin Wall Moure (Art Historian); Mary Parks (Curator), Hallie Ford Museum of Art,Willamette University Salem, OR; Robert Perine (Artist and Writer); Lian Portlow (Librarian and Archivist), Pasadena Museum of History; Adrienne Rappoport, Chouinard Foundation; Michael Redmon (Director of Research), Santa Barbara Historical Society; Tracy Robinson (Reference Archivist), Smithsonian Institution Archives; Lisa Scharnhorst (Manuscripts, Special Collections), University Archives, University of Washington Libraries, Seattle, WA; Jim Schmeltzer (Chairman of the Art Committee), First Unitarian Church of Los Angeles; Millicent Sharma (Librarian), Pasadena Public Library; Patricia Simpson, First Unitarian Church of Los Angeles; Stephanie Spika-Fox (Long Beach History Librarian), Long Beach Public Library; Mary Sprague (President),California Federation of Women's Clubs; Burda Vandeborne (Librarian, The Art, Music, & Recreation Department), Los Angeles Public Library; Kim Walters (Library Director), Southwest Museum; Louise Wexler (Artist); Robert Winter (Architectural Historian); Kim Woo (Librarian), Frances Howard Goldwyn Hollywood Regional Branch, Los Angeles Public Library; Helena Wright (Curator of Graphic Arts Division of Information of Technology & Society), National Museum of American History, Smithsonian Institution; Marian Yoshiki-Kovinick, Archives of American Art.

Index